**Also Available**

*Shaking the Tree: brazen. short. memoir. Volume I*

*Shaking the Tree: brazen. short. memoir. Volume II*
*(Things We Don't Talk About)*

*Shaking the Tree: brazen. short. memoir. Volume III*
*(I Didn't See That One Coming)*

Vol. 4

# SHAKING THE TREE

**BRAZEN.**

**SHORT.**

**MEMOIR.**

## That's a Terrible Idea. What Time?

EDITED BY

**MARNI FREEDMAN & TRACY J. JONES**

INTERNATIONAL
*memoir*
WRITERS ASSOC.

INTERNATIONAL

WRITERS ASSOC.

Published by Memoir Writers Press
2801 B Street, #111
San Diego, CA 92102-2208
SDMWA.org

This book is a memoir anthology. It reflects the authors' present recollections
of experiences over time. Some names and characteristics have been changed, some
events may have been compressed, and dialogue may be recreated.

Copyedited by Erin Willar
Proofread by Anastasia Hipkins
Book cover and interior design by Monkey C Media, monkeyCmedia.com

First Edition
Printed in the United States of America

ISBN (paperback): 978-0-9798551-9-1
ISBN (eBook): 978-0-9888882-5-8

Library of Congress Control Number: available upon request

We want to dedicate this volume of
*Shaking the Tree*
to everyone that has ever made a mistake or jumped into mischief
with their eyes wide open. We've been there.

Dear Reader,

As memoir teachers, we have noticed that many people walk around thinking they are the only ones that have ever screwed up, let their curiosity get the best of them, or been the force of wild-child chaos. Not true. As the stories in these pages reveal, walking straight into a trap of our own making is a near-universal experience.

What do we hope this volume inspires?
Share the story you think you cannot or should not tell.
It's not just you.

Happy reading,

Marni and Tracy

# Shaking the Tree, Vol. 4, 2022

## brazen. short. memoir.

# I AM AJUMMA

LINDSEY SALATKA

"How do I look?" I tugged my short permed black wig forward with my fingernails in a last-ditch effort to cover the grays at my temples. I tucked in a few straggly blond strands in the back. I sucked in my stomach and cinched my pink fanny pack tighter, like a corset. I turned away from the mirror to model my ensemble for my husband, one jazz hand up, the other out.

"You look, mm, different," he said.

"I know that," I said, "but do I look entirely sensible? Like a woman with a purpose who has taken a few hard hits in her life and no longer gives a shit if her pants match her blouse?"

I zipped my brown plaid quilted vest up to my chin and then unzipped it again. My pants, a loose black polyester blend with a blue and white floral pattern and elasticized waistband, were a smidge too short. My mid-length pink socks met them where they ended. The sturdy off-white sandals, complete with heel straps, were there too. I pulled the undershirt sleeves down to cover my wrists.

"I think you achieved the desired effect," he said.

"Good," I said, and exhaled. "I'm a little nervous. Is that silly?"

He smiled. "Which part?"

Point taken.

After a few beats where he perhaps searched for the most favorable wording, he asked, "Do you think this is a midlife crisis?"

I paused, thoughtful, as I positioned my full-face pink vinyl holographic visor. "I prefer to look at it as a midlife awakening.

However, if this is how my midlife crisis manifests, you are very lucky." I kissed him. "Wish me luck! Bye!"

And with that, I trounced out the door and down the steps to meet my fellow flash mob-ees.

I flash mob with a group called Ajumma EXP; you might say we have a different mission than your everyday flash mob. We are all middle-aged women and damn proud of it. We are mostly Asian (not me, though; more on that later) and embrace the spirit of the Ajumma, a Korean term used for a middle-aged woman in sensible albeit ill-matched clothing who is spotted elbowing her way through the subway in Seoul or haggling for vegetables, haggling for any purchase really, like a mofo. Ajummas don't take shit, not from anyone. We used to take shit in our youthful prime and took it for far too long—we didn't have much of a choice back then. Now we know better.

My time performing with Ajumma EXP has been unbutton-your-pants-at-the-dinner-table liberating. But it also ushers in a whole host of questions with good reason, questions that are asked of me, and questions I ask myself. I am a middle-aged white woman dressing like a middle-aged Korean woman. If mostly Asians didn't surround me, this choice would be inexcusable. No one understands my history with these women; how could they? Should I expect people to extend grace to me, to pause and consider me with curiosity and joy instead of anger and judgment, for what could justifiably be labeled cultural appropriation?

I go back to how this began. Almost twenty years ago, I moved to Shanghai with my family. The transition was, in a word, rough. I did not understand their culture. I did not appreciate how they communicated or interacted; in my defense, it was hard to decipher. I mistook someone yelling in my face as a sign of aggression instead of a friendly greeting. I could not get used to the bathrooms—the setting for many unfortunate "accidents." I couldn't stomach the driving, which was terrifying and risked a higher life-and-death level of "accidents." I was flummoxed by the yeses that were nos because why not just say no? You're a haggling culture; give me someplace to start! I was often scared for and protective of my children, even though they were probably safer there than they ever have been here. I was frequently overwhelmed and frustrated.

I caught myself storming away from a shopkeeper who wouldn't take twelve more cents off a badly needed box of tissues. I had the twelve extra cents, but I knew they were charging me more than they charged the locals, which angered me. I got hung up on the principle and wiped my nose on my sleeve—for twelve cents.

In retrospect, I think I sometimes behaved like an unhinged person caught on camera refusing to wear a Covid mask at Costco in the early days of the pandemic. But eventually, something happened. I didn't accept everything happening around me, but I slowly began to thrive, in some ways better than I ever had before, when I was more rigid. I loosened my grip on the helium-balloon string of principles and became more comfortable with different ways of existing.

I enrolled my three kids in a Mandarin immersion school when we moved back to the US. I spent a lot of time at the school and made friends with some of the parents. I discovered that I mostly felt more aligned with the Asian parent contingency. They were frugal, spoke their minds, and stopped at nothing to clear the way for their kids to succeed. I got this.

Eventually, I became friends, in person and on Facebook, with some of the involved parents like me, those who ran the carnivals and fought for school improvements. One day I saw a post featuring some of the parents at the school in tightly permed wigs, quilted vests, fanny packs, sensible shoes, and giant full-face visors at the Asian Film Festival Gala supporting the Pacific Arts Movement. They cleared the dance floor and broke into a well-choreographed routine to "Supersonic" by J. J. Fad. My friends could dance! It was incredible. My mind was blown.

I love to dance. If there is a song and a dance floor, or even a small patch of dirt, you'll likely find me grooving on it. I watched the entire video with a huge grin. I don't recall how many times, but it was borderline creepy. Then I tapped Comment and wrote something reeking of shameless desperation very similar to THIS VIDEO IS THE BEST THING I HAVE EVER WITNESSED IN MY WHOLE ENTIRE LIFE!!! I'M SO BUMMED I'M NOT EVEN 1% KOREAN RIGHT NOW BECAUSE EVERY MOLECULE IN MY BEING YEARNS TO BUST A MOVE WITH THIS CREW. WAHHHHHHHHH-HHHH!!!!!!

Soon, I heard a DING! signaling this reply: "Lindsey, the Ajumma EXPerience is not about being Korean. It is about the ferocity of your middle-aged warrior heart. And if you want to be a part of it, there is a visor with your name on it."

I might have cried or peed my pants a little. Probably both—this is how excited I was. (I'm an Ajumma now, so I can say real stuff like that and not care what people think of me.) I had Prime for my perm and Goodwill for my get-up. Sensible shoes I had in spades. I was ready to begin training for my first flash mob.

Earlier, I said I love to dance. However, loving to do something is different from having a natural ability at said thing. When I say I trained for the flash mob, I mean I dedicated tens of hours to get it right. I was not going to be the tall white gal with zero grooves. I already borderline did not belong; I was not going to stand out even more for sucking.

I attended every practice I could make and then practiced the routine in my living room countless times. By the end, my kids knew the moves as well as I did, possibly better. I could hear my husband humming "Supersonic" in the kitchen when I awoke.

The song spoke to me; I was a freak. I was determined to be on the beat, change moves after every four or eight counts, look enthusiastic, and hoot and clap even though my overarching thought was PLEASE, LINDSEY, DO NOT TRIP.

Our first performance was in a movie theatre—a packed house there to watch a film and a Q&A with the film's director as part of the Spring Showcase of the Pacific Arts Movement. I don't remember the film's name, but Sandra Oh starred in it. I do not possess her riveting entertainer abilities, but I badly wanted to blend. To bring the energy to this group of women who deserved it. I think I did bring it. I sprang into my jumping jacks like Tigger. I shook my moneymaker as if I'd never had sciatica. My head itched, but the rest of me tingled with the joyous rush of endorphins. It truly was Supersonic.

Since then, we have performed dozens of times and learned increasingly complex choreography for four other dances. We have rocked grocery-store produce aisles, food courts, and the black-tie gala to raise funds for the House of Korea in Balboa Park.

Every time, I think all middle-aged women should do this. We should dance with abandon. It's our rite of passage. It is what we have wanted to do our whole lives.

After we dance and are chatting with our fans (yes, we have fans!), we often peel off our wigs and remove our visors. Let me tell you, at this age, dancing in a wig and vest gets hot! But then again, so does everything. While I'm not always the only Caucasian performing in the group, I'm usually the only one with long blond hair bursting forth from my wig. I see looks of shock. Whispers. Sometimes the people I've been talking to pause to decide how they feel. Is this okay?

I've asked myself this same question on many occasions. I asked Lee Ann Kim, Ajumma EXP co-founder, and my friend, this question not long ago.

"Lindsey," Lee Ann said. "This is what inclusion looks like. We are not here to showcase how we are different. We are here to say we are all worthy, and in middle age, dammit, we are all the same."

Therefore, it is with pride that I celebrate my Ajumma spirit, expressing my gratitude for reaching middle age here or anywhere. Some have said that middle age ushers in shame and, with it, expensive potions and procedures, injections, and lifts. How do I rid myself of the fat, burn off the fat, ice off the fat?

We Ajummas snort at vanity. We're too busy getting through our list of errands, telling off jerks at work or the market, and caring for our kids and parents, to be concerned with a few well-deserved wrinkles and dimples. Plus, why spend the time, energy, or money to reverse an irreversible process? Let's embrace our middle age instead. Embrace it and wave our hands in the air like we just don't care, for this is our new, improved prime. And it's a beautiful thing.

# OUT OF TOUCH

BARBARA HUNTINGTON

I spent the morning of my seventy-fourth birthday doing what I did every day during the COVID-19 pandemic: scrolling through Facebook on my phone. Thank goodness I had made so many friends. With each "Happy Birthday" post on my page, I picked an emoji and pasted in the words "Thank You!" Again and again. Damned arthritic hands! I used my thumbs, then right hand, then left. My fingers ached, but my heart hungered even more for acknowledgment that I still existed, that I had not become some gray-haired ghost rattling around an empty house. I pretended a Facebook algorithm did not remind people to send a birthday greeting, or even that the personal message might have been conveniently set to be sent automatically years before.

As I responded to the thirty-seventh "Happy Birthday," a text notification flashed at the top of my screen.

*Still planning to come by this afternoon. Is that okay?*

It was from my daughter-in-law, Ashley, ever concerned about my welfare; how did I become so lucky to have her in my life? I chalked it up to the smart, compassionate son I raised.

Maybe it was a bad idea, their coming over for my birthday, but we would be outside, all wearing masks. We'd done it a couple of times before, and Ashley was extremely conscientious and knowledgeable, so even though I had become increasingly worried about letting down my guard, I hesitantly agreed.

That birthday morning, I had crossed out another day of isolation on the calendar—104 days alone—104 days since I had touched or had been touched by another human being—104 days wondering if this is how I would spend my last days on earth.

As I lay on the couch and scrolled through birthday wishes, I thought about how I had attempted to fill those 104 days: the gluten-free sourdough starter languishing in the refrigerator; the tortilla press, arepa-maker, and sacks and jars of baking materials on the dining room table. Those projects that filled my time and my belly during the early days of hunkering down, discarded when they could not fill the endless hours of loneliness.

Tashi, a sort-of border collie and my only companion, looked up from her end of the couch. She'd tolerate a hug, but it was not her thing.

The phone buzzed, this time a real call from my daughter-in-law. "We want to stop by Baskin-Robbins to get some ice cream. Dale thinks you would want Pralines 'n Cream, but do you have a different choice?"

Uh oh!

My mind ticked off the dangers of removing masks to eat, and how to handle plates, utensils. My mouth responded, "Jamoca Almond Fudge."

Baskin-Robbins automatically evoked my late husband. "Thirty-one flavors" was our family's comfort food, Fred's "let's all jump in the car and go" answer to celebrations and tragedies alike, forever stuck to memories of my little kids before they grew up and had kids of their own.

Soon I was enmeshed in Facebook again. I wanted to scream, "Not another cute kitten!" but I watched those sweet videos, another and another and another.

Then Tashi jumped off the couch and ran downstairs to the yard, as I got the text,

*We're in the backyard. Where are you?*

Grabbing a hat, mask, hand sanitizer, wipes, and shoes, I followed Tashi to the garden. Paused at the top of the stairs, I watched my grandson search for his beloved bugs and my granddaughter pick roses and lavender. I felt that grandma thing in my chest that wanted to hug, to love, to touch, to cuddle, and I steeled myself to keep my distance. As I started down again, the whole family came together and sang "Happy Birthday." I held on to the handrail, stifling the urge to race down and sweep them all up in my arms.

Ashley cautiously poured four quart containers of ice cream out of a bag onto the table and backed off so I could pick out mine. She had packed plastic utensils, napkins, paper bowls, and ice and made sure everyone was eight feet apart before we ceremoniously removed our masks and dug in. Ah, a whole quart of Jamoca Almond Fudge. What a good idea!

My son had hinted he had a small present for me, but how could there be anything more wonderful than seeing him and his family?

After ice cream, the grandkids wandered off in the yard, and Dale excused himself to go inside. As he closed the glass doors behind my chair, he yelled over his shoulder, "I'll be right back, Ash. Want to get the camera ready?"

About five minutes later, my daughter-in-law picked up her phone and started filming me. That's nice, I thought, a remembrance of my birthday, and I smiled at the camera as both grandkids joined her.

Then, from the room behind me, I heard Dale say, "Okay, here we go."

Oh, dang, I thought. Are they going to do a cake with candles? Blowing out candles in the time of COVID-19? Disperse all those little prickly satellite particles all over food?

As Dale emerged, I turned around, expecting the worst and planning to smile anyway. Full brilliant white hazmat suit. At least, I assumed it was Dale. White hood, green gloves, eyes barely showing—something out of a science-fiction movie. The Padres mask gave him away. Confused about whether I was about to be offered a radioactive isotope or if he was worried about catching fire from seventy-four candles, I uttered a non-committal, "Look at you!"

Dale held out his gloved hands. No cake, nothing in them.

I blinked. Dale waited, arms wide. What was I missing here?

"You said you hadn't hugged anyone in 104 days."

I just jumped up and yelled, "I love it!" I grabbed hold, closed my eyes, and squeezed tight.

Ashley kept filming, and the grandkids squealed and clapped. Tashi danced around and around. And my son hugged me back.

Folded against his chest, I felt warm and protected. Real, strong human arms encircled me. Days and nights of loneliness flooded to the surface and dissipated as love and impossible joy flowed with my tears.

We stood like that for a long time, my son and I, he in that crinkly white paper suit, I in blissful peace, the world holding still in the moment.

# TAKING MY BLOND DAUGHTER TO A BLACK LIVES MATTER RALLY

JANELL STRUBE

I made us late. The rally started at 3:00 p.m., and I had told my twenty-four-year-old daughter I would be sure to stop work in time to go, but now it was 5:00 p.m., and I was just getting ready. For months, I had been tracking the names of Black lives lost. These people could have been my brothers, my cousins, my nieces or nephews. I believed in the protest, believed I needed to do something, but was afraid of the consequences. Would I feel safe walking my dog after this? Would people be comfortable around me? Somehow, I knew, there would be no going back.

I checked my appearance in the mirror. Black sweater, black skirt, straight hair in a ponytail, brown skin light enough after months of pandemic isolation to appear almost white. My heart began to pound. Taking a deep breath, I called to my daughter, and we left the house.

The sidewalks of downtown San Juan Capistrano were empty. Then we passed a group of Hispanic young men heading back. The rally was over, they told us, but some people were still protesting in the park.

We continued, but inside I was relieved. *All Blacks who protest are terrorists.* It was the voice in my head, the one that has been there since I was five years old when we went for a Sunday afternoon drive to Watts so my mother could see where the riots happened. It was the first time I heard the phrase, *If they don't like it, they should just go back where they came from.*

At the intersection of Ortega Highway and El Camino Real, we faced a surreal standoff. On the Mission San Juan Capistrano side, next to the adobe wall built in 1776, four policemen in riot gear, looking like marines ready to clear Aleppo, pointed their rifles at three Hispanic teenage girls standing on the opposite corner. The teenagers held up a hand-lettered sign. One of the girls, with wavy black hair that fell to her waist, was speaking through a bullhorn.

*You men should be ashamed,* I thought. *These protesters are just children.* But the girl holding the bullhorn was undeterred.

The light changed, and my daughter and I stepped out into the crosswalk. The guns were now aimed at our backs.

"Black lives matter," the girl with the bullhorn said to me.

Hope stirred in my heart. "Yes, our lives do matter," I said.

Immediately my daughter was offended. "That's not what this is about, Janell," she said. She took me to say, "All lives matter."

"I was agreeing with her," I said. *Thanking her, even.*

"She won't appreciate the nuance," my daughter said under her breath as we walked past.

There were perhaps ten people under the shade trees in the park, the homeless people I saw when walking my dog and a few teenagers hanging out on the tables. Not a single Black person, nor a person who looked like an organizer to answer questions. We headed back home.

When we passed the intersection, empty now, anger replaced the fear that had made me too late to the rally. Anger that, once again, I was on the outside. If I go to a Black Lives Matter rally—from either side—I am an inauthentic protester. The young girl on the corner saw a brunette middle-aged woman walking her blond daughter to a Black Lives Matter rally and felt she needed to tell me that Black lives matter. Inside, I was thinking about the baby who was put up for adoption because her father was Black. Me.

My life had not mattered at the point at which I was the most vulnerable. I am the blending of two worlds that, based on skin color, our society has chosen to divide forever. Long ago, I wrote a poem in French that began, *I am not Black; I am not white; I don't want to be gray, the shadow of two worlds that will never come together again.*

When I was three, I learned that I was "the mulatto child that the Strubes had adopted." It was said every time I was introduced to people, to the point that the pugnacious toddler of the earliest photos of me turned into a shy and tearful girl who hid when meeting people. To this day, I have to force down this anxiety when I meet new people.

The Encyclopedia Britannica taught me about being mulatto. We had a version from the 1930s, musty, with yellowed pages and no color pictures. Under "mulatto," there was a whole section about mulattos, quadroons, octoroons. Complete with woodcut drawings of Black people showing the variations in skin color represented by more or fewer dots, and hair twisted in short spikes. There were more names after octoroon, but I don't recall them now.

When I was thirteen, my sister's boss, who was Black, told my parents that they should be teaching me about my culture, so we went to an event held at the university to hear a Black man speak. For an hour, we stood in a line that snaked around the theater. The couple in front of us wore a midnight-blue silk suit and a black evening gown with fringe that trembled in the evening breeze. My mom said we should have dressed up, but we did not have fancy clothes. I do not remember what Reverend Jesse Jackson said, just the line of dark suits, evening gowns, dangling earrings, necklaces, bracelets, and a sea of Black faces. And my white mom, with her white hair that had to be rinsed in vinegar to keep her bun from yellowing, my white sister, and me. Afterward, my mom called her best friend and said that she had never been so embarrassed. That was the first and last time I would attend a Black cultural event.

I have spent my whole life being impacted by race. It is why I was adopted and grew up in a white household. It is why, when children at school asked what color I was, I would say I was silver. Even my brother, born a year after my adoption, learned to say it. It is why my boyfriend was not allowed to date me, and why I made sure to marry a white man and have an even whiter child.

Being light-skinned means that I am bombarded with racism that swirls like radiation in the atmosphere. People assume who you are, or forget who you are, or do not care. I must always be on my guard, and sometimes it is hard to respond with grace and kindness. When I put my house up for sale, my next-door neighbor of eleven years asked me not to sell to a Black person. "It will bring down the neighborhood," she said.

She and I had traded cups of sugar, borrowed ladders, rescued each other's pets. A couple of years before I moved, in my house, eating my leftovers, this neighbor's son had confided that he was facing thirty years in prison for dealing drugs. He was scared, and I tried to encourage him. My neighbor's son lost his BMW, his life savings, everything to stay out of jail. These neighbors did not view their child's criminal behavior as that, calling it rebellion, or being stupid, but they viewed a Black person moving into our neighborhood as bringing down the neighborhood.

I learned every negative stereotype at the dinner table from my parents' friends. Whenever I would say how these things hurt me, my mother would say, "You're not that Black," but the fear of being thought dumb, stupid, lazy, or fat, made me work hard to be perfect, intelligent, hardworking, and thin. I never wanted anyone to lay fault on me for the color of my skin.

We returned from the non-rally rally, and I still didn't know what I could do to protest. But then, one recent evening, my daughter came home from work with a story to tell. An older white man in a business suit had followed a young man into Staples and yelled at him for driving recklessly in the parking lot. The brown-haired young man was wearing a rash guard and board shorts. The old man said, "Take your brown skin back to where you belong."

Everyone thought he was going to attack the young man. My daughter stepped between the two and separated them, and the blond cashier said, "Sir, we don't accept racist speech in here." The man asked the cashier if she was a fucking liberal, and she replied that she was just a human. The surfer did not understand. He was white, tanned from time spent at the beach, but white.

I am proud of my daughter and the cashier for doing the right thing, but inside I am terrified. It is 2020, but it feels like 1969 again, only worse. What if the cops had been called on this "brown" boy? I realized I had not protected my daughter from anything, but she had the courage to step into a dangerous situation. Growing up, my protection lay in retreat. I was a child who had had to learn how to survive alone.

A radio commentator said racism has been hiding in plain sight. It has never been hidden to me, only now there are cameras to expose it and people who will not accept it. But something exposed is something once hidden, and it is time for me to stop hiding in my own skin.

# BIG APPLE, BIG CHERRY, BIG SMOKE

JEN LAFFLER

It was the eve of a new millennium, and I was graduating from college with a goal so ambitious I didn't dare tell anybody about it: I was going to be a poet, a positive kind of poet whose work would inspire the world! Just two things stood in my way. The first, an American classic, student debt. I needed a job that paid real money, right away. Second, and perhaps more troubling, when I tried writing down the poetical masterpieces swirling in my head, only crap came out. I was no Kahlil Gibran; I was beginning to suspect I wasn't even fully me, yet. And so, I pushed lofty, unlucrative aspirations aside, scored one very lucky interview in New York City, and landed an analyst job at a Wall Street investment bank.

How in the world did a Spanish Lit major with zero-to-no finance background manage to acquire a coveted i-banking position? I had landed in a department of true eccentrics. Boss-man Boris fancied himself a great patron of the arts and filled his corner office with paintings and sculpture. His pièce de résistance was a massive cherry-red sculpture of, well, a gigantic cherry, so big it required a personal plinth to support it. None of us knew quite what to make of the cherry. Boris said that's what made it good art.

Wes was a kind and fatherly type, on the cusp of an extremely well-heeled retirement, who'd long since ceased to even try to pretend to do banking work. He was the longtime mayor of a legendary small town in Connecticut (Paul Newman lived there) and he could (and did) tell stories all day.

But my favorite banking misfit was crusty Jack Devonshire, our IT guy, who was *this close* to finishing his novel. Day after day he filled his screen with tiny type that was not code, his inbox soaring sky-high with overdue work requests. Boris proudly enabled this total dereliction of IT duty and celebrated with vodka shots and opera arias when Jack's novel was eventually published to rave reviews.

The fourteen-hour days ticked by (fourteen-hour days because *someone* had to do all the actual banking work, what with Boris busy fondling his cherry and Wes reading both the *Wall Street Journal* and *New York Times* front to back daily). I made margin calls, wrote the world's least insightful credit analyses (it turns out plagiarism's kind of okay once you leave college), and played with my poems, dreaming of a day when something, someone, would call me out of the confines of the teal-upholstered cubicle—

"Hey, Laffler. When are you coming to London to work for me?"

I expertly toggled out of my poetry spreadsheet (like I was fooling anyone) and swiveled around to face the handsomest man in the world, his blue eyes challenging, appraising, taking me in. Max Davies, thirty-six years old, former British Royal Air Force fighter pilot, current head honcho of London Credit, married twice. I'd met him a few times before and had enjoyed the experience; it seemed obvious that any woman would enjoy the experience. He was, technically speaking, hot as fuck. Even a heathen like me, who bought her clothes at the Salvation Army store in Chelsea, could see he cut an impeccable figure in his English tailoring. No gaudy pinstripes, nothing dandy—he just looked . . . fun. Right. *Good.* The body under the perfect suit? Perfect. His bearing (I'm pretty sure it was the first time I'd ever noticed a man's "bearing"), a curious, just-short-of-cocky mix of RAF pilot and genuinely happy, alert, alive person, a rarity indeed in the teal-tinted corporate doldrums! He had a jawline you could eat your dinner off of. And those eyes? Kind, wicked, interested, cool—his eyes were everything. His eyes were the eyes of a very good yoga teacher whose class you should really stop going to because you're just going to fall in love with him and that's not the reason why you're there. *Or is it?*

(Flash forward—*spoiler alert!*—but come on, you guessed where this is going, right? A few years later, while waiting for him outside a club in

Soho, in London, I struck up a conversation with a nice lesbian couple. I shared that I was waiting for my boyfriend, who happened to be a married man—it felt so good to occasionally be honest with strangers. When he finally showed up, striding with that fresh military-confident step, smiling love and naughtiness and relief deep into me, one of those ladies literally fell right out of her chair. I understood completely. If I'd been sitting in a chair, I would have fallen out too.)

I would like to point out that, in the office that day, and in the year that followed, it never occurred to me that I would actually sleep with Max. I knew he was an exciting man to be around, a whip-smart boss, that we had second-to-none chemistry when it came to water-cooler banter. I also knew that his seemingly cavalier invitation to London was my dead-serious ticket out of the teal cube—to Europe, to travel, to adventure, to really living. But it never occurred to me that things would go further, much further, with him. He was married, and I really was that innocent. End of story, right?

Tricky things like visas, accommodations, contracts got sorted out, and at age twenty-two I moved to London and started working for Max Davies. I happened to arrive on the night of his anniversary party, which involved dancing and "fancy dress" (English-speak for grownups wearing costumes *not* on Halloween). I showed up fresh from Heathrow to find Max getting down in a gladiator costume made of what appeared to be actual chain mail, muscled legs and buttocks bare to the studded codpiece. I was also introduced to his attractive brunette wife, Jillian. I don't recall her costume, but I can still feel how very different her energy was from his. Max's magnetism radiated out, drew in, and included everyone, a friendly force of nature. She was stone cold. When I thanked her sincerely for inviting me to their party, she smoothly (and just out of Max's earshot) replied that *she* hadn't, and she went back to chatting with her friends.

Life in the London office was a blast. Yes, we still worked twelve-to fourteen-hour days, but those hours included copious pub time. We celebrated every birthday, every anniversary, every coming and going; we were "down the pub" every day. This office was big and full of bright international people. My officemate was a delightful Sikh woman named Dipal who, when I complimented her delicious

Indian cooking, took it upon herself to bring me lunch every day. Our long days working together frequently culminated in long nights out together. I was having the time of my life getting to know all my coworkers, including, of course, Max.

Look, no one knows better than me how inappropriate, not to mention immoral, this all sounds. Max had been married twice and had four children; he was fourteen years older than me; he was a "big boss," his star rising within the international bank. He drove a Ferrari, for fuck's sake, and not the kind you just go to the dealership and buy; a custom one, the kind Saudi princes buy. I was twenty-two, in a foreign country, six thousand miles from family. I still wore thrift-store rags; it had kind of become my look. I hadn't driven, much less owned, any kind of car in six years. And yet, we seemed to have everything in common. Not in a creepy, older-dude-cultivating-young-girl kind of a way, but in a—am I really going to say this out loud?—in a soul mate way. This outrageously handsome Englishman who had it all, and plain fuzzy little me, the unpublished poet from Kansas City . . . we could not stop talking to each other. We could carry on an entire conversation in *Wayne's World* or *Austin Powers* quotes. We'd talk politics, history, travel, ideas; our pasts, futures, dreams. Sometimes, in the midst of these conversations, we would find ourselves just looking at each other, communicating nothing and everything with our eyes, and get stuck there, until one of us would have to walk away.

Eventually, he took me out flying in his airplane (he called it an "aeroplane"). He read my poetry and was both warmly supportive and bluntly critical; the harsh hatchet of his criticism was always, maddeningly, right. Finally, one London summer night, after yet another electric night out with the team, we shared a cab home . . . and he never made it home.

Our affair lasted three years, and I think it's safe to say it broke every heart it touched. We didn't make it, his marriage didn't make it, and he ended up losing his job, too.

I take that back. My heart didn't break. To quote a really useful British phrase: I was shattered.

And over time, those shattered shards of my heart grew into poems.

Poems that dared a fresh take on the oldest cliché of them all: true love. Poems about connection so strong it transcends norms and customs, boundaries and definitions, maybe even reality itself. Poems about betrayal so cutting, tawdry, ugly and deliberate, it could literally make you sick.

Poems about lifelong damage.

Poems about forgiveness.

Maybe, someday soon, I'll be brave enough to show them to strangers.

# THIRTY BUCKS

KATHLEEN A. MCCABE

"Hey, Mom, it's me. I've tried a couple times; I guess you're on the phone. I'll try again later."

I got released from jail this morning. They always let you out at zero-dark-thirty, don't want anybody to see you, I guess. I've been in and out a lot this past year. It was forty days this time. They're trying to get me into rehab, but I guess I haven't been very cooperative. Last time, my probation officer actually took me straight there from jail. But I saw a guy who'd fucked me over, and I got into a fist fight. Didn't think they'd take me after that, so I just ditched out the back.

"I had to settle a score," I'd told my mom. She was pissed, I could tell on the phone. She really thought I'd make it this time.

But she held back. I already knew what she was thinking, but "I love you, son. I hope you will make better choices," is what she said. And then she told me what was going on with my little sister, my stepdad and stepbrothers, my gramma. She always tries to keep me connected to the family.

Four days later, they picked me up again. It is a game the Portland cops play, picking up the drug addicts who live on the streets—teaching the new cops how to tell if we're high. Catching us with paraphernalia or enough dope for our next fix, then putting us back in the slammer.

Inside, it's cold turkey. Can't sleep, sweats, jitters. The guys are good to me, help me get through it. Most are older, with kids at home and a wife to hold down the fort. Some have girlfriends who write big messages to them on the sidewalk out front; we can see it through the windows.

I had a girl once. We lived in Bellingham. She had a pit bull terrier named Fat Girl. I loved that dog. I started buying and selling pit puppies. I was good at choosing them. It was going along pretty good, between that and my pot sales. I even bought a car, a Honda Civic. But my girl got nasty. She started using meth and moved in with somebody else.

It was downhill for me after that. She'd introduced me to cocaine, and I loved it. When I ran out of money, I started selling all my shit. All my fish tanks. I had a good rock collection and sold that too. Even the car, gone. My friends got scarce; they were moving on with their lives and stayed away from me. I was stuck in this hole.

I moved back home for a bit. Mom made some rules, and I was doing okay. Got a job at a new restaurant, and they trained me and even gave me a uniform. I started getting tips when the restaurant opened. Cash is not a good thing for me. A really bad thing, truth be told. Pretty soon, I was dabbling; before long, I was falling. Mom kicked me out, bought me a ticket to Portland. "Don't come back unless you are clean and sober."

I know she loves me. She just wants me to get better. She's been through this before, with my dad. He went down and stayed down. She took me and my sister to California when we were little and never looked back. I feel bad that I'm putting her through this again.

I run solo now. I have tons of friends, don't get me wrong. And girls, never any scarcity in that department. But it's enough for me to keep up my own habit, much less theirs. And I won't pimp them out; I'm better than that. I'd rather go without than hurt someone.

So, I've been in Portland a while. I get by. I pick up the odd job, washing windows, parking lot attendant, shit like that. A little low-level dealing to keep me in dope. I live in a hotel sometimes—pay by the week. And I have a dry spot near a church when I'm living outdoors. There is always plenty to eat; you'd be surprised what people throw away. And there are soup kitchens when I want something hot.

I call Mom again. She has an 800 number; she says it's for business, but I know it's for me. This time she answers. "Hey, Mom, can you help me out? There's a BeerFest on the waterfront. I can get work setting up, but I need steel-toe shoes."

I know she's looking it up on the internet while we talk. She does that—checks my stories. I've had to get much better at it, and sometimes they're true. Like today. I've already talked to them; I was there at dawn. But they said to come back with work boots. Mom sometimes helps me out.

"Did you check the thrift stores? Can't you borrow some?"

I knew she'd ask. "I've already been to all of them. But Payless Shoes has them for $30."

She looks up the store online and verifies the price. "Call me back in a bit," she tells me. She'll call them and see if she can pay for them over the phone. They won't let her; I already know that.

I am making my way toward Pioneer Square when I see my buddy. "Dude, what's up?"

"Short Dog, haven't seen you in a while, like more than a month."

"Yeah, they sprung me today."

"Thought that might be where you were. Heh, I'm scoring today; want in on it?"

*Fuck.* I know where he's going. It's the footbridge overlooking the flea market. There is always somebody there with something to sell: junk, coke, meth, a few other things I won't mess with. Hell, I've even done it myself a time or two to earn a score.

It's been forty days since I've used. I'm jonesing, no doubt about it. I'm lined up for another rehab, but my PO can't get me in till four days from now. I really screwed up last time, I know I did, by getting in that fight. I don't want to disappoint my mom again.

I've thought about it a lot since then. I even wrote letters to a few friends about it while I was inside. "I'm about to make some big changes in my life," I told them.

"Glad you are getting clean. I'll be right behind you."

And I mean it. I can't keep doing this to myself. To my mom. I'm twenty-five years old. I'm tired of the rat race, tired of the hustle. Tired of the merry-go-round. I am going to work today, pull some money together. Get into a program and clean up my act.

I get to the Western Union and call Mom again. She sends me the money, and I head up Alder Street toward the shoe store, saying, "Later," to my friend.

I look at the $30 in my hand. Cash. *Nirvana.* The ultimate rush of euphoria, and after that, total peace. No worries, no cares, no hassles.

I turn around and call after him. "Sure, what time?"

This will be my last time, I tell myself. My. Very. Last. Time.

The police visit my mom the next day. "Your son's body was found," they tell her, "in a hotel in Portland." I never imagined that an overdose would be the reason it was my very last time.

# ON THE EDGE

KIMBERLY JOY

The hot tropical sun and humid air of Guam's jungle pressed heavily on me like a blanket. I stood in an opening among the palm trees, staring into a cave's dark, massive entrance—the mouth of a yawning giant. Inside, excited whoops were followed by long gaps of silence. What were they doing in there?

I was twenty-three and had been living and working at a resort in Guam for the past five months. Scuba diving with sharks, bungee jumping, and trekking through the jungle on our days off were typical. My grit and love of a thrill usually had me keeping up with the guys in our other escapades, but this time felt different. A queasiness in my stomach had kept me rooted in place when the others had run into the cave five minutes ago. The sensation reminded me of when I'd stick my hand into a garbage disposal to retrieve something without unplugging it first.

Tim, a good friend and fellow worker, ran out of the cave, cheeks flush. "You've got to check this out! There's a huge hole in the back of the cave. We're throwing sticks into it. It's so deep, you can't hear them hit the bottom." His excitement was contagious, and my curiosity began to override my fear. Almost. I hesitated.

"No, I'm good out here."

"Come on. It's fine. You don't want to miss this," he said, coaxing. My insides twisted even more, but my mind told me that I'd taken risks before; why not again? I was just becoming acquainted with the warning signs of my intuition and had not yet learned to heed them. I took a deep breath for courage and replied.

"Okay, let's go!"

Tim and I stepped from the bright, harsh sunlight into the shade inside the cave opening. The heat of the jungle was replaced by cool, damp air. Standing six-foot-three, Tim helped me feel safe. He walked by my side as we started toward the back of the cave.

"Be careful," he said as he reached out and took my hand, his large hand engulfing mine. "It's pitch black back there, and the opening is just a big gap in the ground. Don't get too close."

He was right about the darkness. As we inched forward, the light from the cave entrance faded like a flashlight whose battery was dying, growing dimmer and dimmer. My steps slowed to a shuffle, and dust coated my sandaled feet. My eyes blinked rapidly, trying to adjust to the almost complete lack of light. After a few moments, I could make out the darker silhouettes of the other boys in the group, standing at the edge of a cavernous opening. The hole was large, probably ten feet by ten feet. It opened up from the back wall of the cave. The back and left portions of the opening met the vertical walls of the cave, but the other edges of the hole were wide open where the ground abruptly ended, spilling into a black vortex of emptiness.

I let go of Tim's hand as we stopped beside the group. One by one, they were taking turns picking up sticks the length of their arms and almost as thick, and throwing them over the lip of the dark, ominous opening into its abyss. I heard a whoosh as a stick was thrown, then nothing. No sound of it hitting bottom. I wondered how deep it was, conjuring up images of black holes and empty wells.

Another stick was thrown. I heard the whistling of the branch as it flew through the air. I strained to hear more, automatically leaning forward and taking a step with my right foot. I yelped in panic. My foot met only air, and I fell forward. Gravity, lightning-quick, sucked me toward the hole.

Tim's large hand slapped my left shoulder blade as he grabbed my thick white T-shirt. His hand pulled hard and fast. I spun to the left. My chest and arms slammed against the cold, hard stone as I landed in the shape of an L, my upper body flat on the ground at the edge of the hole, my legs dangling into the vast darkness below. Tim yanked on the back of my shirt while his other hand grabbed my right arm and heaved me up and out of the opening. I lay face down on the dirt with my head turned to the left, my ear pressing into the earth. My heart hammered against my chest. The sharp metallic taste in my mouth was as if I'd bitten into a copper penny.

Stunned silence hung thick all around me. Then a cacophony of voices overlapped, frantically flying at me.

"Are you OK?"

"What happened?"

"Jesus, Kim, you almost died!"

To my shocked system, they felt like bats swooshing over my head, attacking. I lay there for what felt like hours but was really only minutes. Tim crouched beside me, the back of my shirt still gripped in his tight fist. He pulled to help me stand. My legs trembled, so he half supported and half dragged me toward the cave opening.

"What were you thinking? I told you to be careful," he yelled, his anger masking his fear. His words were muffled over the roar of blood in my ears.

We stumbled out of the cave. I flinched, slapped by the bright sunlight. The muggy heat of the jungle felt suffocating. Tim let me go. I dropped to the ground and sat with my legs curled to my chest, arms around my shins, and my head resting on my knees. I huddled there, rocking back and forth. After a while, an awareness of my body and surroundings returned: the racing of my heart, Tim standing next to me, birds singing.

"You OK?"

Tim's voice broke through the last of the fog in my brain. I lifted my head to examine my body: blood flowing from a cut on my knee, long scratches along my shins, a bruise already forming from my right elbow to wrist. My palms stung from slapping the rough rocks at the edge of the pit. My pride stung as much as my palms, but miraculously, I was unharmed.

"Yeah, I'm OK," I replied.

The rest of the group had emerged from the cave and congregated a few yards away. Over time, their muted conversation grew more animated. Bursts of laughter and high fives erupted. Tim looked in their direction.

"You ready to go?" he asked. I stood slowly, wondering if my legs would hold me. I looked down. My once-white shirt was now covered with brown dirt. My hands swept down my T-shirt again and again, trying to remove the last reminder of my fall as Tim and I walked over and joined the group.

Someone said, "You almost died in there! Are you okay?"

It had all happened so fast; I'd hadn't yet processed that I really did almost die in what would have been a horrific way. I had never thought of death as something that could find me. I was young, healthy, and out conquering the world. I didn't want that feeling to change, to feel vulnerable or scared, so I replied in my bravest voice, "Yeah, I'm fine."

"Cool, because we're going bungee jumping tomorrow. You in?"

My breath caught in my throat, and my stomach turned over, giving me another chance to listen to my intuition.

"I'm in! What time?"

# DID THAT REALLY HAPPEN?

CHILI CILCH

My eyes blinked open, squinting at the morning light peeking through the blinds of my bedroom. *Ugh, my tongue feels like sandpaper.* I pressed my hands to my temples to ease the ache of my throbbing head. I rolled onto my back to stretch, seeing a heap of pink satin and tulle at the foot of my bed. *What the fuck? I knew I shouldn't have swallowed that pill.* I threw a pillow over my face as I recalled my evening. The wedding ceremony, the mad scramble for the keys, granting wishes to strangers downtown—*and had I really kissed Sam?*

This was my seventh wedding, and although the first will always be special, I couldn't imagine another wedding being more extraordinary. I had been officiating nuptials since 1991—almost three years. Ordained by the Universal Life Church, I'll never forget receiving my minister's license and the booklet that came with it explaining the founding church principles, *Freedom, Food, and Sexuality.* I had found my religion. I was in my early thirties, and my family wasn't impressed. My sister, who had just gotten married, taunted me by singing, "Chili keeps marrying, and marrying and marrying, but never gets married herself," riffing from the musical *Gypsy.* Sure, I wanted to get married, but surprisingly, this outrageously extroverted gal pivoted to painfully shy when it came to men I found attractive. Most of the time, I couldn't even muster up the courage to say hello.

I had met my clients, Henry and Jocelyn, at Balboa Park's Prado building to plan their costume party wedding.

"What will you be wearing?" I asked them.

"Antony and Cleopatra," they answered in unison.

Later that night, I pondered, *what am I going to wear?* Deciding on my outfit was always a concern, given that as an officiant, I'd be front and center in the wedding pictures. I had an idea. Having cleared it with the bride, and securing the rental, it was settled. I would be Glinda the Good Witch from the magical land of Oz.

A week later, as I waited for the wedding to start, I admired my reflection in a full-length mirror. *It's perfect.* A pink hoop-skirted gown, wavy red wig topped with a spectacular Lucite crown, and a wand.

I watched, hidden from the second-floor balcony, as Anthony and Cleopatra made their entrance into the courtyard, throwing gold coins to their guests. I then descended the staircase amidst bubbles floating down upon the wedding assembly to the orchestration from the *Wizard of Oz.*

At the part of the ceremony where I asked the couple to exchange vows, in my most Glinda-like voice, I declared, "I now have a very important question for each of you." Turning to the groom, I asked, "Henry, will you be a good husband or a bad husband?"

"I'll be a good husband," Henry answered, laughing, and Jocelyn promised to be a good wife. I pronounced them married, and the happy couple sealed their vows with a kiss to uproarious applause.

I felt elated that the ceremony went so well. I didn't flub the vows or soil my beautiful dress. In my relief, I imbibed a bit too heavily from the cascading champagne fountain. The entire wedding party was dancing, and I was enjoying the swoosh of my dress as I spun in circles. I remembered waving to the groom, Henry, across the dance floor. He flashed me his warm smile. He was busy distributing special "party favors" to some of the guests. He danced over to me and whispered in my ear, "Do you want some?" It was a narcotic, let's call it E. I hesitated. Then an inebriated thought struck me: *Drugs never seem to do anything to me. So why not?*

As the summer light faded, costumed guests danced merrily to the wedding DJ's tunes. *Wait, I know that DJ; it's Sam.* The stark white of his sailor costume reflected the warm glow from the setting sun. About five years earlier, a girlfriend told me that Sam had had a crush on me.

I considered him with renewed interest. *Umm,* I thought, *that white uniform contrasts nicely with his skin.*

I'd forgotten about the little pill. It took about an hour to cast me in its spell, proving my wayward notion incorrect. I was not impervious to drugs. I felt myself swirling in an E-tornado that dizzily landed me inside a magical place.

I felt energized by the E. Colors were brighter, and I felt like I was floating. I found everyone and everything enchanting. After what seemed like thirty minutes (probably closer to three hours), I noticed most of the guests had left. Folded tables and stacked chairs waited for transport. My E-muddled brain queried, *How am I going to get home?*

"I'll take you," Sam offered. I looked at him with E-inspired arousal. "Thank you kindly, captain."

His dark hair curling about the sailor's cap looked adorable. *He's so cool,* I thought, climbing into his Volkswagen van with all my Reverend Glinda paraphernalia.

"This is it; thanks for the ride home." He nodded and parked in front of my place. *He has nice lips.* I leaned in and French kissed him.

"Wow," he muttered, surprised. "I'm sorry I can't hang out; I have another gig to get to with my band."

I smiled and waved my wand around his head. "See you soon." I was too high to remember he had a girlfriend.

I climbed up the stairs to my place and dug into my purse. *Oh crap, where are my keys to my place? Did I leave them at the park?* In the early nineties, people still had landlines; only celebrities used chunky, primitive cell phones. I went to every apartment with residents that knew me, but none of them were home. A light was on in Apartment 9. I rang the doorbell. An attractive couple in their late thirties opened the door. They had recently moved into my complex. Their expressions were appropriate, considering Glinda the Good Witch stood greeting them.

"Hi, I'm your neighbor; my name is Chili. I'm locked out of my apartment; can I use your phone?" They invited me in and offered me a seat on their white sofa. Their whole apartment was gleaming white.

*Be normal, be normal, be normal.* I didn't want them to realize how high I was flying.

"I left my keys at a costume party wedding."

The woman handed me their cordless phone. *Ring, ring, ring, why isn't he picking up?* Finally, my brother answered.

"Hi Kenny, I left my keys at the park. Can you close up the store and come get me?"

Thirty minutes later, my brother rescued that poor couple from my ramblings, about how my junior high English teacher had me ordained, that I had once asked Bill Clinton to do his Elvis impersonation, and that my next wedding would be performed on top of a tank.

*Please be there.* I hunted in the dark, praying that I'd find them. Then I noticed that the DJ table was still set up, and right on top, the keys!

*Thank you, Jesus.* I grabbed my keys and ran to my brother's idling car.

"Kenny, I don't feel like going home; take me to the store." My father owned what I'd call an old-fashioned curiosity shop—filled with books, antiques, and a museum that featured slices of San Diego history, including pictures of 1950s burlesque queens.

"Chili, is that you?" I was surprised to find Billy greeting me inside my dad's store. A tall, lanky photographer, Billy and I frequented the same music clubs. He seemed completely unfazed by my get-up.

I steadied my crown to look up at his face. "How convenient that you're here; I need an escort. Come walk with me around the Gaslamp."

Walking around the historic heart of downtown, I waved like a queen greeting her adoring public. Throngs of people enjoyed the warm evening. Couples on dates, drunken frat boys smoking cigars, and girls in short skirts huddled together, out for a night of clubbing. They greeted me with either enthusiasm or cautious disdain.

"Look, it's my fairy godmother; grant me a wish!"

"And what might your wish be?"

"A red Maserati."

I smiled and waved my wand. "Your wish is granted, my child."

Returning to the store, Billy bid me adieu with a deep bow. "Farewell, my Queen."

Adjacent to the store was an art gallery. On weekends, they transformed their storefront window with butcher paper and backlighting to create a stage for shadow dancers. One male silhouette that looked to be nude was moving slowly, provocatively. Entering the gallery, I stole a peek at the dancer. He winked. "Care to join me?"

"I'd love to." I gathered the pink tulle of my gown and took his extended hand. He kissed my hand, and I curtsied to a faceless audience. What an end to my evening. Dancing with a completely naked man who knew his way around a hoop skirt.

Pulling the pillow from my aching head, I knew that yes, *I really did kiss Sam.* Tongue sandpapered, jaw spasming, and legs aching, I made a solemn vow, *I won't be doing that again.* And yet, somehow, I did not regret taking the E. It gave me a taste of fearlessness.

*If I could glide down the streets in full Glinda the Good Witch regalia, what couldn't I do? Tonight, I think I'll go to the Whistle Stop bar and actually say hello to that cute bouncer.*

I smiled, stretched, and clicked my bare heels together at the thought.

# EXPLODING VALENCIA

LENORE GREINER

The birds of Valencia had wisely fled.

As we emerged from this Spanish city's train station, massive explosions rocked its streets. Trundling luggage, we waded into crowds and chaos as cherry-bomb blasts and drums punctuated the air. Frying churros and gunpowder assaulted our nostrils. As we negotiated the swirling mobs, marching bands blocked the path to our hotel.

We plunged into the clamor of weaponized silliness called Las Fallas Festival, an anarchic celebration of creativity and rebirth. Once a pagan rite of spring, Las Fallas today burns winter away every March 19th on Saint Joseph's feast day.

"Yeah," a former resident had warned us, "don't plan on sleeping much."

"We're here!" hollered Rob over the din.

"It's your dream come true!" I yelled back. Rob had been intrigued ever since we had watched a documentary on this age-old fire festival.

"Where should we go next?" I had asked as we chose our next adventure. "Italy?"

"I really want to go to Las Fallas," said Rob, smiling. "I want to see the bonfires and everything getting blown up."

"Sure you don't want to go back to Italy, to Perugia, and see where your grandfather came from?" I said, even though I wasn't ready to travel there.

"No, I really want to go to Las Fallas."

I'd been shooting for Italy with trepidation. My shoulders slumped as I went hard and cold inside. As a teenager, during a cold year in that hill town, I had been sexually assaulted. My intuition told me to return, confront ancient, anguished memories, and heal. I always believed this violation had been all my fault, that I must've done or said something to cause it. A twisted belief common among rape survivors.

During my last two trips to Italy, feeling broken inside, I lacked the guts to face my devils, the hard memories, my inner incendiary emotions. To blast my life apart again felt unbearable.

Maybe Perugia some other time.

So off to Spain we went. If only we had known what awaited us.

After checking into our hotel, we strolled outside, serenaded by abrupt explosions that jolted and spooked. We watched the locals ignite whining rockets, fountain sprays, and fireworks. Soon a pall of smoke as thick as a San Diego wildfire hung over the old Roman quarter. Wandering the streets with a smile pasted on my face, I found paradise.

In the main square, the Plaça de l'Ajuntament, we spotted our first falla, a fifty-foot-tall effigy of Moses. La plantà, or placement of the fallas around the old Roman quarter, had happened overnight. Now garishly colored figurines, some two stories tall, bloomed in every plaza and intersection—fanciful cartoonish caricatures, such as Elvis or Oprah, or fairytale and Disneyesque characters. Many made satirical or political statements, including Moses himself, commenting on a Spanish banking crisis with a tablet inscribed with the eighth commandment, "Thou shalt not steal."

Valencia's fallas began as a pagan rite of spring when debris piles appeared outside homes and workshops after spring cleanings. Bits and pieces were transformed into playful figures or symbols and then set afire in community bonfires where people gathered to dance, drum, and sing.

Today constructed of wood, Styrofoam, paper, and wax, the Valencians had stuffed over 700 fallas with fireworks and gunpowder—each creation astonishingly flammable, each destined for a fierce end on the festival's final night, La Cremà, the Cremation.

Over five days, we awoke to brass bands marching below our window at 6:00 a.m. We explored streets that shook with heart-stopping blasts. We dodged rockets whistling past our heads. We danced amid the staccato bursts of sizzling firecrackers thrown at our feet. Every night at 1:00 a.m., we joined the throngs to watch fireworks blossom over the Turia River. Then we'd collapse dead asleep in our beds as detonations sounded all night long.

During our days serenaded by dynamite and fireworks, we eagerly awaited the climactic night when Valencians would almost burn their city to the ground.

One lovely spring afternoon, we dined on fragrant paella and chilled sangria on shady Plaça de Rodrigo Bortet. We could hear the 100,000 revelers packing the square roar as fierce artificial earthquakes called terratrèmols rocked under our feet.

A better choice than Italy, for sure. Maybe I'll never get to Perugia. Maybe I'll never get over what happened there.

"This was such a great idea," I said to Rob.

He didn't hear me. The Valencians were busy vaporizing 110 pounds of gunpowder and four tons of dynamite in the main plaza during the daily mayhem called La Mascletà.

"Oh my God, Rob, look," I said. "That dad is showing his kid how to light a firecracker with a cigarette. She's gotta be only three years old."

Cherry bombs drowned out his reply. Some boys had just set off a deafening symphony of six blasts in an alleyway for better amplification. Armed and dangerous, children ran around holding matches, sacks of fireworks, and lit cigarettes. Around our table, young kids held lit sparklers and dodged a whistling, crackling fountain spraying the pavement with sparks.

Finally, Las Fallas' fiery finale, La Cremà, arrived. To end this part-pagan, part-religious, part-civic fiesta, Valencians lit their fallas afire until 700 bonfires raged all over the old Roman quarter.

That night, we joined jovial mobs fanning into the streets, pushing closer toward the intense heat to watch explosive pyrotechnics set the fallas ablaze. Firefighters blocked off intersections to battle conflagrations licking as high as three stories. Water cascaded down the sides of apartment buildings and waterfalled over shop awnings into the gutters.

At one in the morning, we dodged snaking fire hoses and followed the crowd to the main plaza for the incendiary climax. Locals lit long ropes laced with firecrackers, which raced toward the mighty Moses. A swift, flaming hell of fireworks encircled the colossal falla, detonating the bombs packed inside. As his insides ignited, his eyes glowed menacingly red. Then, a giant flame burst out of the top of his head, a flame licking higher into the sky than the eight-story hotels lining the plaza.

Behind me, I heard an American voice.

"They would never allow this in New York City."

I ascended a light pole to better view the inferno.

"God, I can feel the heat up here."

Rob didn't answer. He could not. He was spellbound.

From my perch I wondered, why come to Valencia and not Italy?

Watching the blaze, furious and burning yet warm and illuminating, I realized I was holding on tight to my trauma. Why? Because it made me who I am today? Because I was so young? Because I didn't know what else to do.

Can I walk into the conflagration awaiting in Italy? Allow the fire to purify me, cleanse me? Reduce my old pain into an insignificant ash pile that disappears in the wind?

Suddenly, the misshapen black structure of the former Moses collapsed into a glowing heap as the roar of bulldozers fired up to shovel the wreckage and ashes.

The quieter revelers—families, children, and international visitors like us—slowly dispersed, leaving gutters awash in beer cans and the paper shards of exploded firecrackers.

Back in our hotel, we fell into an exhausted sleep as bombs and rockets boomed through the night.

The next morning, I awoke to a bizarre din.

"What's that sound?"

The buzz of traffic had reclaimed the city. Instead of raucous marching bands, city buses ran across the main plaza, executives purposely strode down the sidewalks, and the banks had reopened for business. Schoolchildren headed off to school; their parents had probably returned to giving warnings about not playing with matches. The remnants of bonfire embers had been cleared from the streets.

In the main plaza, workers swiftly removed gray piles of ash, charred wood, and twisted, blackened wire where a colossal Moses once stood.

Shell-shocked and deaf, stuffed with paella, jamon iberico, and churros, battle-weary travelers departed for the train station.

Sadness crossed my face as I studied the scene outside our window; Valencia is now another ordinary European city.

"It's as if Las Fallas was all a nonsensical dream," I said. "All faded by morning."

Valencia had created and destroyed its whimsical fallas to expose, ridicule, and incinerate the darker side of life, a necessary cleansing, a bona fide purification before spring's arrival.

Mission accomplished.

I sat down with a happy spouse for our morning coffee, saying, "Sometimes you just have to blow everything up. And then you can find a sort of peacefulness."

I realized my new mission—a return to Perugia. I can blow up years of PTSD, and then, I'm certain, my world will surely return to normal.

Outside our window, I heard trilling in the trees.

"Listen," I said. "The birds have returned to Valencia."

# LUNCH WITH MY HUSBAND'S LOVER

## M. ANNETTE KETNER

My office phone woke me out of deep and troubling thoughts.

"This is Helga. I'm calling to ask if you would be willing to meet me for lunch on Friday to discuss my relationship with your husband."

"I think that's a terrible idea. But what time did you have in mind?"

I hung up the phone screaming, "OMG OMG OMG!" What did I just agree to? Meeting my husband's girlfriend for lunch? What's the matter with me? For heaven's sake, how do you have lunch with your husband's girlfriend? What kind of questions do you ask? "So, is this long-term, or do you have a time limit in mind?" Or "Did it ever occur to you that this man you find attractive has two wonderful little children who need his love and attention more than you do?" Or "What in God's name were you thinking, you Badword-Badword-Badword Person?"

Or do you play it cool and say, "I assume your moral principles have come to the surface, and that's why you are here today." Or "I am aware that 70 percent of married men have an affair at some time during their marriage, so I'm not surprised to hear this. I'm just surprised you have the nerve to meet me for lunch."

Or do you just shut up and listen. And see what happens. Why is there no "how-to" book on this, like *Fifty Reliable Responses When Dealing with Your Husband's Lover?*

By the time that rainy Friday rolled around, the lump in my stomach had grown to the size of Yosemite's Half Dome. I was at a distinct disadvantage since I had just learned about this affair the previous Saturday night when my husband didn't come home from a house closing. Desperate by 2:00 a.m. and fearing there had been an accident on the slippery winter roads, I had called the home of Helga, his coworker, to trace his last whereabouts. Instead of Helga, her husband answered gruffly. After listening to an obscene tirade which included calling his wife a whore, I realized something had been going on that he was aware of and I was not. I was still in shock and denial, trying to answer a million questions that all began with "Maybe that's why . . . ."

After ten years of a pretty okay marriage, there I was, sitting in the cafeteria of my office building, far across from the entrance, wondering if I would even recognize this wretched person that had suddenly upset my entire world. All I knew was that she was blond and her name was Helga. *What kind of a name is Helga, anyway? Swedish? No, that's Heidi. No, that's Austrian. Maybe German? Probably. That would make more sense. Maybe she will recognize me, and I won't have to do anything.*

After what seemed like an eternity, the door opened, and a smallish blond woman wearing large turquoise sunglasses walked in and looked around the seating area, gave a slight wave of her hand, and approached my table. There was no sun. It was raining California cats and dogs. Maybe the sunglasses gave her a sense of protection between herself and a difficult conversation.

*So, now what do I do? Stand up? Shake hands? Glare angrily?* My heart pounding, I raised slightly as she pulled out the chair across from me and plopped down heavily.

"I'm Helga."

"I know."

An awkward silence followed. Not the last one of the afternoon, to be sure.

"I thought it would be good if we had a talk."

"So, what's on your mind?"

"I wanted you to know that I never intended to hurt you or the children. I just found Donny attractive, and as we worked closely on different real estate listings, we began to have a lot of fun together. He has such a great sense of humor, you know."

Oh, yes. I knew. Among all my husband's attributes, his sense of humor was one of the things that had drawn me to him in the first place. He would come into my father's restaurant when I was working years ago and greet me with, "Hi Sunshine, how's the world treating you today?" And then tease me about something silly but sweet. Oh, yes, I was well aware of his sense of humor.

She went on, "Before long, we were staying late, after the office closed, to talk about different possibilities for the people we were working with. It all started so innocently. Just friends, you know."

Yes, I knew. Donny had told me about his colleague and that she had good ideas about which houses would be of interest to which of their clients. He told me she would go with him to show the properties, and her people skills helped the buyers and sellers. Yes. I knew about his friend Helga.

"And after the closing last Saturday, we went for a drink to celebrate, and it turned into something else. I'm sure you have heard the details by now."

No, I had not heard the details. Nor did I think I could bear to hear them now. I got the gist of it, and sometimes, the gist is all you need to know.

She took off her sunglasses. I gasped. OMG. The sunglasses weren't there for their usual purpose; they were there to cover a really deep purple-and-red black eye.

She continued. "My husband set me straight when I got home at 3:00 a.m. He said, 'Either you quit your job and never see that son-of-a-bitch again, or you can pack your bag tonight and get the hell out of my house.'"

I could hardly breathe, imagining the scene and the violence that occurred. I was now beginning to feel sorry for her, of all things.

"I'm staying with him. He is the love of my life. I just got distracted a bit. So, I have quit my job. I told Donny it was over. And I'm here to apologize for what I've done and let you know it won't happen again."

To say I was at a loss for words would be like saying fire was hot or water was wet. Of course, I was at a loss for words. What in the world do you say at a time like this? Why was there no book!

There was again this deep and solemn silence. It may have been the black eye that got me or the sight of my son's and daughter's faces marching through my recent memory, asking, "Why isn't Daddy coming home for dinner again tonight?" But without any direction from me, tears began pooling in my eyes. I could understand. Nobody intended to cause such great pain to so many people. The fact that I had gone to the attorney on Monday to draw up divorce papers now seemed a bit anticlimactic. Was it worth disintegrating a whole family for a mistake made in the heat of the moment? I knew what that meant from my parent's divorce when I was fifteen. Divorce doesn't solve any problems; it just creates new ones and an upside-down world that never regains its balance.

After what seemed like an eternity, I said, "Well, thank you for coming. And thank you for the decision you made."

She quietly responded, "I wish you well. You have a wonderful husband, and he truly loves you and the children. I am so sorry."

She put her sunglasses back on, stood to go, and hesitated a moment. I was at a loss over what to do next. So, what I did was a surprise to both of us. I gave her a hug and said, "Goodbye. I hope we never see each other again."

As I watched her walk out into the pouring rain, I knew why there was no "how-to" book. You can't prepare for some of the things life throws your way.

Sometimes you just have to simply shut up and listen.

# DJ LOVE

## JON BLOCK

"You got to quiet that voice in your head, man. It's destroying you."

*What voice is this asshole talking about?*

"That voice," Ray said. "I call him DJ Hate. Every track he spins in your head, man, it's hate. Hate for everybody, especially you."

*What's Ray blabbing about? Fuck this; I'm getting another beer. Fuck that; I'm leaving. Fuck that; I want a cocktail first.*

\*\*\*

The past year was rough. I told people I produced music and arts events for a living, which was true except for the last part.

My last four events had been horrendous flops, and I was borrowing money from my parents to stay alive, a fact I loathed about myself.

In fact, self-loathing had become a superpower. When my event-promoting peers had a successful event, I felt like an epic loser. When I caught my volunteers slacking, in my mind, I called them "lazy shit-for-brains," then judged myself for being an ungrateful asshole.

I was a month away from turning thirty. I was committed to becoming financially independent and being seen as a respected professional. I saw myself getting married in the next five years and being a solid provider.

It was time to grow up.

So that's why my next event was positioned to be my most lucrative yet.

\*\*\*

I was co-producing InterdepenDANCE, a music and circus festival with Burners Without Borders, a nonprofit composed of Burning Man devotees. Our event was scheduled for the July 4th weekend at Balboa Park. We had gotten the venue free of charge, and the Burning Man community would attend in massive numbers. They did not care how much money they pocketed for their organization so long as we threw a great party, a fact which greatly supported the Jon Block relief fund.

I blocked out three months to focus exclusively on Interdepen-DANCE. I was feeling optimistic and excited nine days out, as Ray, the head of Burners Without Borders, and I met with the planning committee to present the final details.

"When the festival ends at 11:00 p.m.," I said, pointing to the PowerPoint timeline, "we have twenty volunteers who will immediately start breaking down the three stages and eight installations."

"As Burners," Ray humbly added, "we practice a 'leave no trace' principle to respect the land. So, the park will be in even better shape after the event."

I smiled as we let our preparedness sink in. Ray and I had gotten to know each other fairly well these past three months. He was five years older than me, with thinning red hair and a mellow temperament that was a welcome contrast to my high-strung nature.

Yet at this moment, we both noticed it was taking a very long time for anybody from Balboa Park to say anything.

Finally, Leah, a woman in her seventies, spoke up.

"We googled 'Burning Man' and saw a very disturbing YouTube. Naked in the desert, on God-knows-what substances, and . . ." She trailed off as if completing her thought was unbearable.

" . . . Orgies!" her husband Frank spat with revulsion. "There is NO WAY we are hosting a thousand drug-fueled sex addicts at our village!"

Frank put a manly arm around his wife as if he had successfully defended their home from hoodlums. I tried explaining this event would be fully clothed, respectful, and drug-free (okay, that last part was a stretch), but it was useless. The event was dead, taking down with it months of preparation and forty thousand dollars in lost income.

After the meeting, Ray and I went to the closest watering hole.

"Those motherfuckers," I began, ranting about how they had completely dicked us. Then about how they were too closed-minded to see the benefits of our event traffic. Then about how we should sue them for breach of contract. Send them a video of our naked orgy on the yacht we purchase with their settlement money.

Then my finger-pointing geared inward.

"I'm such an idiot." I exhaled. "Worthless fucking idiot."

And that's when he said it: the sentence that changed my life.

"You got to quiet that voice in your head, man. It's destroying you."

*What voice is this asshole talking about?*

"That voice," Ray said. "I call him DJ Hate. Every track he spins in your head, man, it's hate. Hate for everybody, especially you."

*What's Ray blabbing about? Fuck this; I'm getting another beer. Fuck that; I'm leaving. Fuck that; I want a cocktail first.*

"Yo!" I waved to the bartender. Ray pulled my arm down.

"I know what it's like to be angry. I was that way all my life."

"Good for you," I said. "Bartender!"

I waved my arm. Ray slammed it down on the table.

"DJ Hate is saying nasty things all the time," Ray continued. "Probably saying nasty things about me now, right?"

There was no point in denying that one. I nodded.

"DJ Hate got so bad for me, I came *this* close to killing myself to make him stop. That voice was relentless. Always telling me, 'You're broke,' 'You're a loser,' 'You're a fuck-up.'"

Hearing Ray talk about DJ Hate, I realized for the first time that this voice might just be something separate from me.

"How did you break free from it?"

He told me about a three-day self-development seminar. That was disappointing; I was expecting to hear something cool like skydiving or taking ayahuasca.

The next day I called their office, telling the guy who picked up the phone that I thought self-help seminars were for suckers and scam artists. Then, to my shock and amazement, I paid $500 and registered for their next event.

***

Friday morning, as the course started, I was convinced I'd made a mistake. The format consisted of the instructor teaching a concept; then, among us ninety participants, we could volunteer to explore how the concept related to our own lives.

I understood some concepts but did not see how they could launch me into "proper adulting." Other participants went to the microphone and cried buckets, and you could feel decades of weight lifting off their shoulders. I developed a mounting case of breakthrough envy.

*Where's your breakthrough? Huh?!? You invested three days and 500 bucks you don't have. Make it happen, bitch.*

I rubbed the sides of my face, trying to quiet my inner voice. It was very distracting to have a voice telling you to have a breakthrough while you're trying to have a breakthrough.

"There's a voice inside our heads," the instructor said, "providing a running audio commentary of our lives. The voice sounds just like us. But have you noticed that it tends not to say nice things to you?"

*This* captured my attention.

The instructor drew two circles on the board. The left circle was called **Fact,** and the right circle **Story.**

The thesis was that, as people with hyperactive minds, we create meaning out of everything. From our money situation to our family members to the number of pounds we weigh, we have an opinion on *everything*. Our opinion was referred to as our "story" about it, and it was usually a negative one. And in a cruel twist, the closer we got toward making positive change in our lives, the fiercer these negative stories became.

I sensed something important was brewing. I raised my hand; the instructor sent me to the microphone.

"I'm thirty years old," I began. "I graduated from USC for screen-writing, never made a penny in Hollywood. Now I produce music and arts events. People think I'm successful. Truth is, I'm horrible at making money."

I hesitated, then figured I'd already come this far.

"I can't get it together. It's like I'm cursed."

For the first time, when it came to my failures and finances, I did not sugarcoat, present half-truths, or defend myself.

The instructor drew my attention to the two circles on the board.

"From everything you just shared, what are the facts?"

He tapped his chalk against the first circle.

"I'm thirty years old," I answered.

"Go on."

"I graduated from USC."

The instructor nodded.

"I produce events."

The instructor nodded again, encouraging me to continue.

"I'm horrible at making money."

"STOP."

*Fucking idiot, I can't do anything right.*

"You just said, 'I'm horrible at making money.' Is that Fact or Story?" The instructor tapped the first and second circle, respectively.

"Take a look at my bank account," I told him. "It's a fact, Jack."

"Are you sure?"

"About my bank account? Sadly, yes."

"The amount of dollars inside your bank account is a fact. Yes. It's data. I'm asking about being horrible at making money. Is that Fact or Story?"

I stared at him. Then at my empty chair. Maybe this was a rhetorical question I was meant to sit with. I half-stepped toward my seat, then these words darted out my mouth:

"Holy shit, it's my story."

The participants chuckled.

"What else is your story?" the instructor asked.

"That I'm cursed," I answered immediately. "That I can't do anything right. That it's always gonna be this way."

I was gathering steam.

"None of it's true," I declared. "I can be anything I say I am."

Was I wrong? I'd experienced so many I-finally-got-this-moments in life that had turned out to be only the illusion of progress. Was this yet another case?

*I can't believe you're falling for this shit. "I can be anything I say I am?" What is this, a Disney cartoon? You came here to grow up, remember? You stupid fuck.*

I paused, hearing DJ Hate's words. Time slowed down. For the first time, I felt there was room now. Room to choose a story that actually supported me.

"I can be anything I say I am," I repeated.

The instructor nodded at me, then looked at the participants:

"We call this transformation."

***

Three days later, I called my event volunteers and apologized for how I spoke to them, acknowledging their willingness to give their time.

I called my event-promoter peers to congratulate them on their productions in a way that only someone who'd also been through the trenches could express.

I called Leah at Balboa Park and told her I respected the committee's decision to do what they felt was best for their space.

From then on, the purpose of my events changed, with two values making up my North Star—personal transformation and community. The same two guiding values I hold to this day. My own transformation has been an ongoing practice; seminars are to my mind what the gym is to my body.

And although DJ Hate may still blast a track now and then, his sets are always cut short. Mostly he's in the background, barely audible.

# MUSTACHE TWIRLING

MARLA L. ANDERSON

I think of myself as a levelheaded low risk-taker, which normally works to my benefit, but occasionally what I see in the rearview mirror shatters that self-image. Such is the case when I reflect on my decision to help a friend. This friend, Susie, is kind-hearted and generous. I can count on her for help when I need it and entertainment when I don't. She's a drama queen who lives under a cloud of improbability better suited to a Hollywood script. It's morbidly fascinating, kind of like a traffic accident.

When she asks me, "How are you?" I say, "Fine."

When I ask her, she says, "My dog died, I'm getting a divorce, my mother has Alzheimer's, my sister's dying, my daughter hates me, my son's girlfriend is pregnant, and a kitten got stuck in my car's engine," and then she describes it all in such vivid detail that I could prepare a transcript documenting the entire event.

One day, she tells me about her brokenhearted daughter, Amy. Now poor Amy, who is already emotionally distraught by the fact that her husband has left her without explanation, recently discovered that her wayward husband tricked her into signing a second mortgage financed by a friend of his. The husband is now missing, along with the proceeds from the loan, which is in arrears, and this friend of his is trying to evict her.

"What?!"

Tears streaming down her face, Susie has my attention. She says her daughter is nearly suicidal and fears that if the house is lost, her daughter may be lost as well. But fear not, Susie has a plan. She will get a new loan to pay off the nefarious villain and save her daughter.

"Really? How?"

Turns out that Amy and her mother have high-paying jobs, and Susie has enough money in the bank for the down payment. Well, almost enough. She just needs another $10,000, and would I be willing to make them a short-term loan? *That's a terrible idea. Never loan money to a friend.*

"When do you need it?"

Suzie's mortgage broker has my name now. The loan's ready, just waiting for the transfer of funds. Just one problem—the bank has decided Susie's credit's no good. She had a rough patch where she fell behind on some payments, plus she recently changed jobs and doesn't meet the six-month minimum the bank requires. She needs a co-signer, or the whole thing will fall apart. Would I be willing? *That's a terrible idea. I would be liable.*

But Susie and her attorney present me with a signed agreement holding me harmless from all payments on the loan and any costs that might be incurred, and with Amy's house as my collateral. The numbers add up with room to spare. *Doesn't seem like much of a risk.* And Susie is desperate to save her daughter from losing the house and her mind, or worse. I've known her daughter since she was little, and I'm a mother, too.

"Where do I sign?"

The loan goes through. Susie and her daughter make the monthly payments, and all is well until Amy's roommate moves out, and now she can't cover her part. No problem, Susie will pick up the slack until Amy finds a new tenant, which should be fine. Except it's 2008. The housing market bursts, and we're entering the worst recession since the Great Depression. There is no new tenant; Amy's income dries up; Susie gets laid off; the mortgage is in arrears. Rather than watch my credit go down the toilet, I make up the difference, but it's unsustainable. We have to sell fast. Unfortunately, Amy is having none of it. The daughter, who Susie was convinced would lose her mind if she lost her house, is proving her mother correct. Amy locks the doors and won't answer our calls.

Meanwhile, housing prices continue to nosedive. Amy and her little dog are now squatters. The landlord needs to evict them. *Oh my god, that's me! How did I become the dastardly villain who throws damsels out on the street?* But it's my future on the line, and Amy doesn't care. I must embrace my inner villain evilly twirling a mustache. This is war.

Now I should probably hire an attorney, but why be out more money? I'm a retired law office administrator with paralegal experience. *That's a terrible idea. Even attorneys shouldn't represent themselves.* I dive into the rights of landlords and tenants. Soon an inch-thick stack of paperwork sits before me, and I think, *Oh lord, what special hell is this?* I push on. I fill out the forms, pay the fees, follow the rules, then wait. It takes months, but finally, the day arrives for the sheriff to meet me at the house to evict Amy. She's had months to figure this out. I'm hoping she's left, and taken her little dog, too, but I've brought a pet carrier just in case. Her mother isn't here. It's just me, my husband, the sheriff, and a locksmith.

When the sheriff knocks on the door, Amy answers in her bare feet. She looks at us with wide eyes and complains no one told her. She sits on the ground and begs. I shake my head in disbelief. *I'm Snidely Whiplash.* Amy refuses to cooperate and won't restrain her dog, so we put it in the carrier while the sheriff proceeds to serve eviction papers. Amy sobs and says she has nowhere to go. I remind her that her mother invited her to live with her. She has options. She says she doesn't. The exchange is useless. The sheriff insists Amy leave, and finally, she drives off in her car with her dog in *my* carrier.

His duty done, the sheriff leaves, the locksmith goes to work, and my husband and I go inside to determine the extent of the damage. To put it mildly, we are unprepared. We've walked into an episode of *Hoarders.* There is stuff everywhere: dog poop, rat droppings, rotting food, overflowing bins, and scattered trash. The master bedroom is so full, it's difficult to tell where the bed is, and the sliding door won't open, and there are holes in the walls, and *oh great*, missing tile in the bathrooms, and a busted toilet. Our realtor plans to show the place tomorrow. My husband (who doesn't say "I told you so," even though he did) and I start cleaning—bagging up dog poop, rat droppings, spoiled food, and trash. We push aside stacks of boxes, magazines, and clothing to carve passages from one room to the next.

Meanwhile, the locksmith is outside changing the locks. I hear someone retching and find the locksmith doubled over in the yard. An open door to a storage area below reveals piles of mildewed clothes. I apologize. He says not to worry. We all go back to work. He continues retching. I try not to listen. After a while, the retching ends, and he knocks at the front door to hand me a set of new keys and an invoice. I thank him, pay him, then go back inside to tackle spilled birdseed mixed with rat poop.

When the kitchen starts to look like a kitchen again, we gain access to a hidden door that opens to the garage. We peek inside and discover an impenetrable wall of discarded bedding, towels, clothing, appliances, and more. Packed to the rafters is no exaggeration. We gingerly close the door and put up a cautionary "Do Not Enter!" sign. We go back to cleaning and more cleaning. While I can't claim the house is habitable when we run out of energy, it's no longer a health hazard, and buyers looking for a fixer-upper can at least see what's inside. It's dark out now. My husband, the saint, is still talking to me and still not saying "I told you so."

To my relief, we have an offer on the house a few weeks later, but for half what it was worth before. Susie's down payment is gone, and my name's on the loan, so I'm worried the bank will come after me. My credit is shot. I feel stupid and gullible but won't beat myself up for not predicting the crash. I'm in good company there.

It takes some time, but the economy and my credit eventually recover, and Susie and I are still friends. I haven't seen the daughter since I evicted her, but she and her mother are back on good terms. Best of all, I've never had to take on the role of a mustache-twirler again. I've no idea what happened to the runaway husband or his lender friend. Too bad. I would have liked to have sent them that mustache. Pretty sure it rightfully belongs to them.

# CASABLANCA ASYLUM

NICOLA RANSON

It was 1393 on the Hijri calendar, 1974 on mine. Casablanca is a modern city in the ancient world of Morocco, and I had expected a hospital staffed with uniformed doctors and nurses. However, when I pushed open the door to the asylum, there were no workers to greet me, only the stink of feces and urine. I was nineteen, and the men in the two rows of metal beds stared ravenously at me and my slightly younger cousin, Kate, who had golden-red hair that was like catnip to males. When I saw how many of the men were masturbating, I clamped my mouth shut to keep the vomit inside. Others called out in French, pleading for help:

"Please, go and see my mother."

"Bring us American cigarettes."

We were looking for our friend: "The German, where is he?" They pointed to the next identical ward. We found Kurt, his eyes glazed with medication.

"We've told your consulate. They'll get you home." He was more interested in the crayons we'd brought.

"Don't give him anything," said the man in the next bed. "The workers will take it. They've stolen our sheets."

Crayons were the least we could give Kurt, as I'd been the one to call the police. At the time, I hadn't much cared where they took him.

We'd met Kurt and his friends, Christian and George, in a sleepy village in the south of Spain. They'd driven from Germany where they'd been friends for years. "Come to Morocco with us," they'd asked. "Do the cooking and we'll provide the transport." We liked that they didn't come on to us, plus we had our own tent, so we would be independent. Kate was keen to see Morocco. I was hesitant. My grandmother had been killed in a car accident there. I'd heard about the arbitrariness of their legal system as my uncle, the driver, had been advised to leave the country because his mother was French, the culture of the colonizer. "You don't stand a chance," a lawyer told him. "The driver who knocked you off the mountain is German, so he'll be ruled innocent, and you'll be accused of manslaughter."

However, my parents' warnings didn't stand a chance against the allure of veiled women and cheap dope. I decided that any dangers could be addressed by traveling with some German men. We knew male company was a good idea and these guys were young and safe, with great camping equipment. But the shiny new VW bus was the clincher. It belonged to Kurt, who proudly wiped off every bird dropping. His bus was the epitome of cool.

"We're ready. When do we leave?"

Kurt liked to do most of the driving, and he led us in singing the lyrics to Pink Floyd's "The Wall." We all became friends in the shared discovery of donkeys, camels, and veiled women. Villagers waved as we drove by, and the gas station attendant invited us into his home to eat chicken tagine and smoke hashish. We were blown away, both by the dope and the hospitality.

The next morning, Kate and I woke up to the sound of Kurt hammering in our tent pegs, something he'd begun the night before. Had he been up all night? Then, when we drove into the throbbing traffic of Casablanca and located the campground, Kurt pulled in, then immediately turned around and headed for the beach instead. After all our map-reading efforts. He drove fast and erratically. When Christian tried to grab the steering wheel, Kurt hit him. Hard.

That night, Christian and George visited our tent down on the beach. "We've never seen him like this. It must be the hash he smoked yesterday. Could we trade places and sleep in your tent? He's much calmer around you." In the morning, Kate and I were woken by Kurt's yells.

"Get out get out! The beach is going to explode. You must get out of there!" Half asleep, I wasn't going anywhere, especially as I was in my sleeping bag wearing only a tee shirt. Enraged at my lack of response, Kurt grabbed my sleeping bag and hauled me onto the roadside. Jolted awake, I screamed for help. This angered him further, and he hit me on the head. Something he repeated each time I yelled.

Help appeared as a car moved toward us. I clung to my sleeping bag, and my decency, as Kurt dragged me along the side of the road. "Au secours!" I cried out, and Kurt thwacked me on the head.

"Help!" he shouted.

The car slowed, the couple inside took one look at us, then sped up. Incensed, Kurt let go of me and ran after the car and out of sight. What a relief to have him gone. Our small group, now dressed, tried to make sense of it all.

"The signs say 'dangerous beach'; he must have interpreted that as 'explosive.'"

"I get he was trying to save me—but what the hell are we going to do?"

Kurt owned the VW, and we weren't about to let him drive it.

Half an hour later, he wandered back. Soon afterward, the police arrived with a paddy wagon. They bundled Kurt into the back, and my alarm escalated to horror when they grabbed my arms and threw me in too. I was scared to be locked inside with Kurt, but he was subdued, sunk into his inner world.

"What am I here for?" I asked at the police station.

"That car that drove by you? That was the police inspector. And his pregnant wife. He's charging the two of you with attempting to murder his unborn child."

Everything I'd heard about the Moroccan judicial system surged into my brain. I imagined myself in a rat-infested cell for murdering someone who didn't yet exist, (*if* the woman was even pregnant). What chance did I have against an angry police inspector who didn't bother showing up to accuse us? Kurt didn't speak French, so, as we were passed from official to official, I had to summon my high school skills to speak for him too.

By late afternoon, at perhaps the third hearing in the third government building. I made the same argument I'd been making all day, which wasn't getting me anywhere. At least Kate and the two guys had been able to follow us and were now seated in the courtroom or wherever we were.

"Why did you dirty hippies frighten a pregnant woman?"

"My friend was yelling because he thought the beach was going to explode. He was trying to save me."

"He was obviously high on drugs."

"No monsieur, it's not drugs. I think he's crazy."

"What are you doing bringing crazy people into Morocco? You filthy kids who swim naked in our sea."

"Monsieur, he wasn't crazy until we got here."

Eventually they dropped the charges against me, but I stayed to speak up for Kurt until the judge threw up his hands and told us to get out of there. Which solved one problem, but what to do about Kurt? Out of options, I went back inside to speak to the official. "Monsieur, he needs a doctor. Please help us." For the first time, he believed me, and he gave me the name and address of a German-speaking psychiatrist.

The doctor handed us a bag of pills. "Give him these, and keep him away from marijuana. The crisis is yet to come." What was he, a psychic? Kurt let Christian drive to the campground where I could begin to exhale in a green oasis surrounded by fellow travelers. Our little group maintained a distance from others, guarding our shared problem. But now Christian and George were reluctant to be around Kurt, so Kate and I felt responsible for looking after him. Try getting a large uncooperative man to swallow pills. We attempted to make sense of Kurt's inner world, which came out in the drawings he scrawled inside his formerly pristine bus. Illustrations of Moroccan landmarks along the route we had planned to take together.

A few days later, Kurt grew more agitated. He started to remove items from the bus and strewed them around the campsite. Had he stopped the pills? Or smoked dope? Kate and I returned from a walk to find clothes from our backpacks flapping from a tree. "He's getting really weird," said Christian. "Says he has to take the bus apart."

By the time we went to sleep—fully dressed—Kurt had removed the car seats. Around 2:00 a.m. he started yelling as he ransacked the inside of his bus, searching for something: "Where is the axe? I need the axe."

"Why do you need the axe? It's time to sleep, Kurt." Kate knew where we'd hidden it.

His reply was loud and urgent. "I have to kill someone tonight."

A cold stream of terror doused me. I made ready to slowly back away, like you do with a bear. We were too slow. Kurt pounced on us and grabbed a fistful of Kate's hair. I jumped at him and pounded his arm. "Let her go! Let her go!"

Surprisingly, he did. He seemed satisfied with the clump of golden hair in his hand.

"I will burn this. And make babies." He clambered to the roof of the VW and flicked his lighter.

Neighboring campers surrounded our site armed with sticks and flashlights. "He's not an animal in the zoo," hissed Kate. "Kurt, don't be scared." He responded with an aggressive roar.

When the police arrived at dawn, Kurt was still on the roof. As they took him away, he smiled and waved goodbye. "We'll call and let you know which hospital," they told us. They never did. After searching the hospitals, we found him in the asylum several days later.

\*\*\*

It was years before I understood the meaning of a psychotic break. In retrospect, Kurt's behavior was a classic manic episode, possibly triggered by drugs. His consulate did get him back home and his friends flew away. Which left Kate and me in Morocco without a ride.

# FLINGS

LAUREN CROSS

The April after we moved from London to southern Spain, I sat with my new friends at a long table covered with a pink tablecloth on the patio of a sprawling cortijo, a traditional Andalusian farmhouse built around a courtyard. My friends sang happy birthday in English, then in Spanish, beneath a warm spring sky, our faces clustered around the amber glow of ten pink birthday candles. Next to me was my new best friend, Chrissy, an American girl. I knew a bit about the States, having lived in Los Angeles a couple of years earlier. I felt comfortable with Americans. When I'd returned to my school in London, I'd only been gone a year, but so much had changed. One friend's mother had dropped dead of a brain aneurysm. Another friend had moved away. And I experienced culture shock returning to my birthplace. "Foreign Lauren!" my classmates taunted. "You sound American!" And somewhere between moving again—this time, from the damp masonry and green leaves of West London to the dust of the ochre fields of Andalusia—I became aware of my parents' troubled marriage.

It probably started in London, a few months after we'd returned from Los Angeles. A slow afternoon with breakfast plates piled by the sink, still sticky with toast crumbs and balancing marmalade-smeared butter knives. I was playing in my room but stopped when I heard shouting. I looked down from my bedroom window at the glass roof of the kitchen conservatory three stories below. I could see my mum on the phone, waving her hands. Her shouting continued, creeping up the ancient wisteria that connected the brick wall of the kitchen to my windowsill, disrupting my play. I tiptoed across my room to the top

63

of the stairs outside my door and began a slow descent on my bottom, one step at a time, listening to one side of a massive row. My mother was hurling verbal abuse down the phone at my dad in California.

I appeared in the doorway of our conservatory kitchen in time to see her fling a pot of Rose's Lime Marmalade across the room. I watched as the glass jar flew toward the glass walls, its trajectory truncated by the smash of a blue willow print china lamp. The fat grenade shape of the jar remained intact, preserving the preserves inside. It rolled under the table, a conduit for my mother's anger, whose face softened slightly when she saw me peeping in the doorway. It would be another year before I realized I was witnessing the cracks in my parents' marriage.

***

It was bedtime at the cortijo. My new bedroom was at the far end of the courtyard from the main house. My legs were tucked under a white woven bedspread, and I leaned my head against the textured bumps of a concrete wall painted pale pink. My dad came in to say goodnight. He perched on the edge of my bed but didn't turn out the light. I felt mixed up inside, like I should know what was coming, except I didn't. I smelled the sour and dusty green of booze and joints and knew he wasn't there to read me a story.

"Your mother doesn't love me anymore, Lolly . . . and I don't know what to do."

He looked like an altar boy, beseeching the heavens for intervention. He closed his eyes, and his lashes wicked away tears. He opened his eyes and stared at me expectantly, like I should have answers. I was wide-eyed with uncertainty. I wanted to say, "I don't know what you should do—I'm only ten!" but I felt guilty for even thinking that. I felt sorry for my dad. He looked so sad. But I was overcome by a new feeling that I didn't have a word for yet: *helplessness*. To make all the feelings go away, I suggested he buy my mum a ring. She hadn't worn her wedding band in a long time. Isn't that what grownups did, buy each other jewelry? "That's a good idea, Lolly. Go to sleep." He kissed the top of my head goodnight.

Not long after, my mother was sporting a teardrop-shaped ruby surrounded by diamonds on her hand. I was baffled that my dad had taken my advice. But that's another thing grownups did: talk to you like an adult, but treat you like a little kid.

Adults were confusing.

So was puberty.

I was still playing with dolls but had a new secret game. I fantasized about being a mother. I'd dump a mixture of talcum powder and yellow baby shampoo to simulate poop into my baby dolls' tiny diapers. When I overheard my dad sigh about the innocence of childhood, I felt guilty. Like I was lying about what I was really doing—not playing, but *growing up*. I knew I was still a kid, but my body was changing, and I was newly aware of what life beyond childhood looked like, filled with bosoms and periods and sex.

While my best friend Chrissy was already wearing proper bras with adjustable straps and a clasp at the back, I wasn't even in training bras yet—but I had underarm hair, *so there!* An unspoken source of tension between us was who would be the first to get their period. Lately, we had started playing a different game with our Cabbage Patch Kid dolls, Arecelia and Sophie. Our dolls had recently started bragging to each other about how their bodies were changing. Chrissy preened over Arecelia getting pubic hair, and I triumphantly declared Sophie had got her period. After the game was over, Chrissy and I took a bath together. We talked about boys we liked and French kissing. Which boy's tongue would we most like to have in our mouth? We laughed, *ewww!* But we wondered what was it like, so we kissed each other, clinking teeth, slippery tongues and all. I liked it more than Chrissy did. We lay in the bath, scissors-style, our vulvas touching. *Is this sex? We're not making a baby, so does it count?* Chrissy giggled that we were lesbians. *Am I?* I didn't think so. I liked boys; I just liked girls too. I said, "No, we're just practicing." And so that's what we called our first experiences: *practicing*.

On the day I announced I wasn't going to play with dolls anymore, my dad sighed again. His eyes turned skyward for a moment before they rested on me. "Don't be in a hurry to grow up, love. Once your childhood is over, it's over." It was the first time I ever felt irritated by him. But the intensity of his beady eyes, glaring with the sadness of someone who feared he was saying goodbye to his little girl as well as his wife, silenced me. His work would soon take him back to LA. What was supposed to be a couple of months apart would end up being a year, and soon, there was a new man in my mother's life. A Belgian with a fondness for Côte d'Or chocolate and Harry Belafonte.

"We're going to go swimming today," my mum beamed, "with Robert." She pronounced his name the French way, *Rob-air*, breathlessly. She seemed starstruck; her casual pause conferred significance to his being there. We'd been seeing rather a lot of him. Up until that pause, I'd thought Robert was just a new friend gladly showing my mum and her kids around a new country. He had a membership to Coral Beach, an apartment club boasting a larger-than-Olympic-sized saltwater pool on the edge of the Mediterranean. I loved going to Coral Beach. We ate hummus and burgers in the outside restaurant on the beach. After lunch, we'd choose ice creams from a picture menu—anything from a fancy half-coconut filled with coconut ice cream, to my favorite, a vampire popsicle with black-cola flavored ice on the outside and a red jelly interior hiding bubblegum. All day, I'd scamper between the sea and the pool. I'd charge into the cold sea, then run, dripping wet, across the hot sand that squeaked underfoot, along cooler pathways lined with the dark green foliage of low palms and bright flowers that whipped my ankles as I sped past, and then I'd fling myself into the warm saltwater pool. After the stinging currents of the salty sea, the silken pool water tasted sweet. After a volatile marriage, it was hard to know if Robert was friend or fling or . . . .

"Are you in love with him?" I was almost eleven, but I surprised myself with such a bold question. I looked up and met my mother's startled eyes. I didn't look away. The answer stared back at me.

" . . . Yes, I am . . . ." It would have been easy for her to lie. I respected her for not treating me like a little kid, but I felt myself slump. *Great. My parents are getting a divorce.* I wondered if my dad, all the way in LA, knew about Robert too.

\*\*\*

One night I had a nightmare. The skies in my dream were stormy. I heard a man's voice hiss deep in my ear, "A helpless joint upon the floor." I looked down to see a detached elbow lying on the floor by my bed, briefly illuminated by a flash of purple lightning. I woke up to a pitch-black room, terrified. It was raining, so I could hear the frogs in the courtyard. I was a little kid, desperate for her mama. I didn't know what was worse, lying there shaking under the covers or heading across the new-moon courtyard to find her at the other end of the house.

I braved the courtyard, hurrying along its edges. The air was damp with croaking. I tried not to step on any frogs but twice felt the cold squelch of amphibious flesh squeezed between my toes. I didn't stop. I ran into the house, weeping as I felt my way through the dark. I could see the crack of light from my mother's closed bedroom door. It was my North Star, beaming me in. I opened the door and saw the worst thing possible: a perfectly made empty bed. My mother hadn't been there all night. She'd left me all alone. On her bedside table lay her ruby ring. I knew where she had gone, who she was with, and what they were doing together.

When I'd dried my eyes, I picked my way through the frogs back to bed. I was only ten, but I knew things. Grown-up things. And I wouldn't be helpless anymore.

# DOULA

VIN SCHROETER

Butterflies fluttered in my belly as I parked. I carried a large gift bag and sighed as I passed the "Welcome to the Baby Shower" sign. I swallowed my rising sadness, determined to act pleasant. It had been fourteen years since I lost my own babies from ectopic pregnancies. Up until this moment, I had never been able to muster the will to attend a baby shower. That was until my youngest sister, Anita, who was eight months pregnant with her first child, asked me to come.

In a family of twelve children, Anita was the youngest girl, a cheerful little sprite, and thirteen years younger than me. The six older sisters doted on her, listening to the Beatles as we combed her hair and dressed her up. Anita and I permanently bonded the night Dad carried her as a toddler to my bed, saying, "We need room for the new baby, so can Anita sleep in your bed?" We sang the same two songs every night: "Puff the Magic Dragon" and "Side by Side."

***

I stepped into a living area decked out in yellow and pink streamers. I greeted my sister, in a red maternity dress, who was about to open gifts. As the crowd drank mimosas, they got louder, like mocking-birds chattering, and it grated on my ears. I told myself I was going to stay for only an hour. Through a forced smile, I couldn't help but remember fourteen years earlier, when I lay on a cold hospital bed. The tall, dark-haired doctor read the ultrasound to me. "Nope. There is nothing in the uterus and a mass in the fallopian tube. It's nonviable." I shivered as the memory intruded.

I stayed the hour, hugged Anita goodbye, and moved to make my escape. With my hand on the door, I looked up to see Anita waddling toward me. "Vin, I was wondering, I really want you to be in the birth room when I have the baby. Please, will you be there with me?"

Her question took me aback. The truth was, I couldn't imagine ever entering a hospital again. About an hour after the doctor told me the baby was not viable, I felt pain like a sharp knife stabbing my left side. Feeling faint, I was placed in a wheelchair. The nausea rose. I threw up into a plastic bowl as I was rushed to surgery. Shivering, I was placed on a gurney while panic flooded my being. My fallopian tube had burst, filling me with blood from my groin to my shoulders. I was losing my second baby and maybe my life.

I shook my head to be less fuzzy-brained and came back to the moment with my sister. My voice was shaky. "Me? Are you sure?"

"Yes," she replied, confident, hopeful. I saw the vulnerable little girl in her face. I felt panic rise up. I decided to pivot.

"I know; why don't you pick one of our sisters who's given birth, like Peggy or Bonny?" Anita shook her head—*No*. I gave it one more try.

"Then how about Cefe, Maria, or Josefa?" She shook her head no once again.

"Why me?"

"Because you are the one who calms me."

I realized I wanted to be there for Anita as she gave birth; I also worried that my grief would overwhelm me when the time came. The grief, it seemed, had a mind of its own.

"Okay, I'll do it." We hugged.

As I drove away, the sadness invaded me, and I was tumbling. I gripped the wheel just to stay on the road and had to wipe my tears because they made the green, yellow, and red traffic lights bleed together. I thought about the year after that ectopic pregnancy when we adopted our beautiful daughter at just six and a half weeks old. As the tearful birth parents handed her to my husband and me, she opened her blue eyes and claimed our hearts.

It was a dance of sorrow and gratitude.

One month after the shower, Anita called. "I'm all alone. Tim is at work, and I think I'm having contractions." I grabbed an overnight bag. As I drove, I felt a resolved strength, and yet I could hear a low drumbeat of fear. *What do I know about giving birth? What if something goes wrong and I can't handle it?*

When I arrived, Anita was calmer. We sat down for lunch. "I had trouble sleeping last night and have pains I think are contractions. Maybe false contractions?"

"I don't know. Did you ask your doctor?"

"My doctor told me to use an egg timer to measure between contractions. Where did I put that egg timer?" Anita looked through the cupboards until she noticed it on the top of the refrigerator. She reached, then screamed in pain, and dropped down, clutching her belly. I helped her lie down until her pain subsided. I grabbed the timer. As we timed the contractions, she showed me the cross she would hold onto in the hospital. It was made of smooth wood and had rounded corners. I was happy my little sister found comfort in her faith. I didn't really know that about her before that moment. I pulled a rosary out of my purse and showed it to her.

When the contractions were ten minutes apart, I started to get nervous. Trying to sound casual, I asked, "When are we supposed to go to the hospital? Do we go when your water breaks, like in the movies? Or is that too late?"

"I don't know."

I felt this floating sense of being lost in a strange city. We called a nurse but were told she would call back. We needed help, someone who had been through this before. As a last resort, Anita called Susy, her husband's ex-wife, an experienced mother of three. She was at the front door within five minutes. "How far apart are the contractions?"

"The last one, ah, it was five minutes ago."

She looked at the two of us like we were the most clueless women on earth. "Get to the hospital now!" she bellowed.

I put Anita's hospital bag in my car, trying not to show any alarm. Anita gave me directions as I drove. "Drive the back way to the hospital to avoid freeway traffic." I stared at her. I had no idea where I was.

"Okay, just turn left here."

I wound around unfamiliar backroads with too many green trees, and all I wanted was to see a big white medical building in an asphalt city. By some miracle, we emerged back into civilization. I exhaled at the giant red arrow pointing us to the hospital. We parked, and I looked at the double glass doors. Dread hit me. I knew that once I went inside this building, I'd have to walk past the ghosts of my last experience in a place like this. But then I looked at my sister, and a sense of love and purpose steadied my steps. As soon as we made our way inside, relief came over me; someone who knew what they were doing could take over.

She was placed in a wheelchair, and we pushed her down corridors to the maternity ward. The nursery walls were painted in pastels. A wave of sadness hit me. Babies were born here, and babies died here. We entered her large private birthing suite and settled in for hours of contractions and ice chips and monitoring by professionals. Anita's husband arrived. Her friends came and went, and my thirteen-year-old daughter arrived. My daughter was attentive, serving ice chips and cold washcloths. Hours passed. Anita and I were sometimes serious and sometimes silly. I glanced at the fetal and maternal monitor. Nurses popped in and out, but I never left my sister's side.

Then the birth was imminent. We all stared at the clock on the wall. It was July 22, 1999. It was almost midnight. My sister said, "If she just hangs on, she'll be born on my birthday."

At the stroke of midnight, we held hands and began singing, "Happy birthday to you—"

"Stop!" she yelled, as she groaned through another contraction, this one hurting more than the last. Anita looked at the photo of our mother and two grandmothers she had tacked on the wall. "Help me, Mom." The nurses summoned the obstetrician. Through the door strode a middle-aged male doctor with a big, confident smile. He asked a few of us to hold her legs above her knees. I didn't want to, but I did it anyway. I swallowed back tears, seeing my sister in pain while the doctor sat on a chair, looking for the emergence.

I watched my sister's face, but my ears were on the doctor's voice: "Okay, you are doing great . . . bear down now and push . . . very good . . . we have a crowning . . . and one more time, push."

Anita grunted loud and long; her sweaty face strained red; then, I heard this splashy sound. Like in slow motion, the doctor caught a perfect reddish-white tiny being and lifted her up for us to see. I was amazed at this miracle with ten toes, ten fingers, wet brown hair, and a round face. My heart was transformed, and I wanted to stare at her forever. The doctor looked at the clock: 1:30 a.m. Love spread from my head to my toes. I was so happy that I was here.

I was lost, staring at the marvel of this new being, when the baby made a gurgling sound. The crew whisked her into the corner. Anita strained to see, and I wanted to follow the baby too, but my feet stayed glued to my sister's bedside. I told her what they were doing, using my calmest voice. The baby's father peered into the bassinet. He looked her in the eyes. "Hi, Alana." The baby's eyes blinked slowly. Her arms and legs settled as she stared at her daddy.

The next day, I brought my husband and daughter back to the hospital, and we found my sister cuddling her serene newborn. Anita reached out. "I need a picture of you, me, and our daughters." My thirteen-year-old daughter looked down at her chipping blue fingernail polish but smiled. She and I stood over the bed and placed our heads near Anita and Alana. My husband raised his camera and pointed it toward the bed. We all looked at the new baby.

Click.

# TRUTH OR DARE

JENNIFER GASNER

1991, Wisconsin

My eighteenth birthday would mark my first public appearance as a drunk girl with a neuromuscular disease. When I drank, my teetering body got worse. My body would lose all sense of balance. Walking got harder. Even standing got harder. I could've easily broken a bone or hit my head. But I hadn't.

My friends and I had never been to the Option, an all-ages dance club. We wanted to go where Marky Mark or Mariah Carey were never heard. The Option stuck to alternative artists like Depeche Mode, Pixies, and the Jesus and Mary Chain. My appreciation for the genre—which never played on my local radio stations—bordered on obsessive.

While Jon drove, I used a thirty-two-ounce water bottle, complete with a straw, to suck down a mostly-rum rum and coke. Jon had an Elvis-like sneer, and his eyes twinkled. His brown hair was buzzed for the summer. We had become friends during our time at a small, dogmatic Lutheran high school. Almost a year prior, a neurologist had determined my serial clumsiness and lack of balance was due to a rare progressive disease called Friedreich's Ataxia (FA). I walked with a subtle staggering gait with bursts of swerving. Eventually, I would use a wheelchair.

The good Lutheran girl in me considered that I probably shouldn't go. I followed the rules. I thought about Jon being underage and buying alcohol, driving with open containers, and lying to my parents. But the lure of forgetting myself, moving to the beat, and getting absorbed into the rhythm won out. Like nothing else, dancing made me feel as if I had escaped to another world.

I finished the bottle as we parked in the gravel lot of the club. We got out of the navy four-door '80s Chevy Citation. I noticed that everything was out of focus; I could sort of make out the club. My legs felt like Jell-O. I took Jon's sober arm, and he led me to the booming beat shaking the building.

As soon as we entered, a thick curtain of smoke-filled air enveloped us. The flicker of the strobe lights made me dizzy—*why had I not thought this might affect my sense of balance?* As we pushed through the crowd, my feet stammered, and I squeezed Jon's arm tighter. I tried to steady myself and time my blinks with the spasms of flashing white lights, but the reality was I felt like I was on a roller coaster.

Finally, we found the bar, and I held on for dear life as the faces of my handful of friends appeared through the haze. "Happy birthday," they yelled over the music.

My sober buddy, Steve, hugged my body, and I sank into his embrace. Steve, a year older, had brown, tightly curled hair, glasses, and a slightly protruding chin. He was my musical guru and was always in the friend zone despite his desire for more. I wondered if he could smell the alcohol on my breath. He knew I was not supposed to drink.

"Thanks." My body had become more like an invertebrate's—limp with no supporting structure. I welcomed the relief as he held me.

I heard the beginning chant of "Hot, Hot, Hot" by the Cure—one of my favorite songs. The time to abandon my post at the bar had arrived. My heart soared as I signaled to the group to get on the dance floor. I held on to Steve's shoulders from behind, keeping my head down to avoid the shocks of white light.

I tried to stay close to the edge where I could hold onto a rail to steady my body. But by the first round of the chorus, I had drifted away and was lost in the crowd without a safety net.

I didn't want to admit it, but I felt my legs were weakening. The pulsing and flickering seemed to speed up—and now I was inside a whirl of lights and sounds. All I wanted was the room to stop spinning.

Smith squealed, "Hey, hey, hey," and the next thing I knew, my face met the floor.

I lay on the floor like an upside-down corpse. I saw Steve's well-worn tennis shoes rush to me, and he rolled me on my back. My friends' serious faces peered back at me. Worry, panic, fear. My first instinct to laugh at my ungraceful tumble disappeared when I noticed a searing pain pulsating through my left hand.

I pushed myself up as best as I could to a seated position. My torso pitched right. My good hand caught me, and I looked at my left hand. My left thumb stuck straight out from my palm at a 90-degree angle. What had I done?

My heart felt like a jackhammer in my chest.

My breath stopped.

"Get me out of here," I managed to say.

Steve pulled me to my feet and put my arm over his shoulders to support me. We stumbled out to the gravel parking lot.

"Your thumb might be broken. We have to do something," one of them said.

"Oh no. I can't go to the hospital. I can't. There's no way to explain this to my parents." A wave of sobbing rose, and I couldn't contain it. The pounding in my thumb was only intensifying.

I fell into the backseat of the car, my head now swirling, my stomach turning upside down.

Outside, I could hear Steve raging at Jon. "You know she's not supposed to drink that much. How could you let this happen? Did you encourage her?"

Shaking his head in concern, Jon drove me home to my worry-prone mother. I scrambled to figure out an excuse for my misshapen hand and unsteady gait that didn't involve underage drinking.

Mom stared at me in our kitchen—concern all over her face. I tried to stand upright, even though I felt I might throw up. "The lights totally messed with me," I said. Her face relaxed. She bought it but still grabbed her keys.

"Okay, but we must go to the ER to check it out. Let's get in the car." While I knew I had to go, I was relieved that she hadn't figured out I was drunk.

We settled into the exam room. By now, I was completely sober. My mom perused my chart and said, "It should say 'fallen down drunk,'" holding back a chuckle.

I looked at my mom. I looked at my hand. For the first time, I felt how different my life would be because of FA. Even though I had the diagnosis, Friedreich's Ataxia had just been words. They held no concrete meaning to me. But from that moment on, I realized that wherever I went, I'd need to consider if there would be bars I could hold on to and chairs to sit on, the lighting, and my own equilibrium. My disease would always be there, telling me what I could and couldn't do and surprising me with its brutal honesty. We left the ER. I had learned my lesson.

Until a month later in a sweaty basement, when I happily accepted the red Solo cup filled with beer—hanging onto another stranger, my world out of focus, if only for one night.

# THE WATERMELON

JANET HAFNER

Dirty-white aluminum hangers lined one side of the runway at the Carlsbad Municipal Airport. Small single-engine planes, a fraction of the size of a jumbo jet, waited in front of their homes. Some looked like they wouldn't make it off the ground, while others looked like they were fresh off the production line. Since this was a first for me—flying in a two-seater—I wasn't sure what to expect. My stomach tightened. *Nothing to be anxious about; he's flown for forty years.* As I walked through a six-foot-tall metal gate, he popped out from behind one of the newer models. "Just in time."

I hoped this weekend would be as great as he promised. I hadn't had time off all year. I imagine forty-eight hours to sit on the beach and have my fill of fish tacos and cold beer. Two firsts: flying in a single-engine plane and hanging out in Bahia de Los Angeles, a sleepy village on the Gulf of California. Lots of palm trees and vendors pushing carts selling mangos. "Oh, Gene, this is going to be the best vacation."

"Climb up and fasten your harness. Put on these headphones. You'll be able to hear me better." A moment later he asked, "Ready?" My heart danced in time with the propeller. "You'll like this," he said, in a confident voice.

From a purr to a roar and then to a thunder, the engine rushed us toward the end of the runway. His weathered hand advanced the throttle. He pulled back on the control yoke and the nose tilted up. *Oh my God.*

"The nose is raised about five degrees. Increases lift from the wings—gives us liftoff." The plane quivered as it took its natural position in the air. I could almost hear it whisper, "Finally."

Below us: all of San Diego. The beach looked like it had just stepped out of a travel magazine. "There's Balboa Park and the zoo, and wow, the Coronado Bridge is so long." With precision and grace, Gene gently banked the aircraft to give me a better view. Fear had stayed on the ground, replaced with awe.

The expansive deep blue to my right had no end. Cargo ships were grains of rice.

Hours passed as the humming drone of the engine and the sun's roasting rays shining through the Plexiglas windshield melted all my tension into an empty calm.

Then, a crackle in my ears. "We got a late start. That's not good."

"Hmm," I whispered. Apprehension had tinted his voice. "What does that mean?"

To the left was a long body of water bordered on both sides with near-white sand.

"That's the Sea of Cortez," Gene said, above the hum of the engine. The sky slipped into a palate of orange, gray, gold, and purple. The plane tilted to the left, the nose pointed down, and the sky lost its color.

"Are we here? Is this our final destination?" I scanned the landscape: nothing but dirt, rocks, and sand—miles and miles of rough sand.

"We gotta get out of the air. We've got to land. We'll be in a world of hurt if we don't." Alarm traveled through the headphones. I looked out the window.

"What do you mean 'world of hurt'? What are you talking about?" The words stung my tongue. "Landing's a terrible idea," I said. My stomach knotted. "No airport, no landing field."

"See if you can find it." Gene's tone sent static through my body. My fingers rolled into tight balls. Nails dug into palms.

I cleared my throat and said, "I don't see an airport anywhere. What am I looking for?"

"No, no, not an airport. You're looking for a windsock, a long cone-shaped cloth that fills with air. Find it. We need it to land."

"There's nothing but sand and brush. The light's almost gone." My tongue stuck to my dry lips. My breathing sputtered.

And then I saw it—a pole with a wind-battered funnel-shaped dirty white scrap of cloth.

"I see it. There it is, Gene. On our right." The plane came around to where my index finger pointed. "It's not a runway. It's nothing but a strip of dirt. Are we—" Before I could finish my question, grains of sand had become visible. The Cessna eased down and gently bumped along the dirt airstrip. It halted inches before the brush. *Damn, he's good at landing. Hardly felt a thing.*

"There." Calm returned and, with it, a smile. We sat in silence.

"We had to land before sunset. It's the law," he mumbled. "Mexican law requires all foreign aircraft to be out of their sky before sunset. No exceptions," he said. "But—"

The corners of his mouth changed direction. Small wrinkles formed between his eyes. Something had his attention. I turned my head to find what he was staring at.

Two headlights and two searchlights barreled straight for us. A cloud of dust engulfed the vehicles as the driver slammed on the brakes. My body rumbled in time with a heartbeat I didn't recognize. I couldn't imagine what was happening.

Six military-garbed men waving machine guns leaped out of the truck. They pounded on the side of the plane. My nerves shook with the plane.

"What are they going to do to us? I've heard stories of people being locked up and forgotten in Mexican jails. Oh God, what should we do?"

Gene was a silent statue.

"Get out of the plane!" the men shouted in Spanish. Gene didn't move. I wanted to shout back in Spanish but couldn't think of what to say.

"Gene, we have to get out of the plane." I jabbed his arm. They bellowed at us again.

We scrambled out of the plane and stood close to it. In front of us stood five fully armed Mexican policemen. The one holding a machine gun had slits for eyes. His downward-turned jet-black mustache framed tobacco-stained teeth. His finger slid on and off the trigger. The others were holding pistols.

"Get on your knees," the leader shouted. Spanish flew at us. "What do you have in your plane? You are smugglers. Give us what you have," the insistent voice yelled. "We're police. Give us what's in your plane."

"We're here—" sputtered from Gene's lips, but the soldier cut him off, raising his rifle as a warning. He roared about smuggling.

I found my Spanish and stammered, "We're here for the weekend; we aren't smugglers."

"What do you have? Show us what you have! Give it to us now!" the officer with the dense black mustache demanded. The other policía shifted from side to side, fingers on the triggers of their guns. The smell of stale beer made me gag. They had had so much to drink that two of them swayed.

They insisted. I swore. Nothing I said impressed our captors. Gene was silent. *What are you thinking? Do something.* Then, without a word, he turned, took two steps toward the Cessna, and opened a small compartment door on the side of the plane. I couldn't believe what he did next. Half of his body slipped inside the plane while his legs dangled, and his toes fought to stay connected to the ground.

"Alto, alto!" the one in charge screamed.

"Gene, stop! What are you doing? They're going to shoot you," I yelled.

Shouting erupted. I could feel my face scrunching tight so my eyes wouldn't see what was about to happen. One soldier stepped so close to me that I could smell his sweat. The others ran after Gene, who had pulled most of his body out of the little cavern he had dived into.

"Gene!" I wailed. "Please don't shoot," I begged the policía.

"Come out of there. I'm going to shoot," barked the leader. He cocked his weapon.

Not a moment too soon, Gene fully emerged, holding a giant watermelon. Yep, that was it—all he was holding was a watermelon. The jefe's anger turned into rage as he screamed, "What else do you have in there?"

In English, I screamed at Gene, "What are you doing?"

His arms stretched out, cradling the large watermelon. "This is for you," he said quietly to the boss, "for you." I translated. Gene lingered.

The jefe looked confused. I was bewildered. The boss inched closer. He hesitated then reached for the watermelon. Two steps back, an about-face, and he was in the truck. The others jumped in the back. What remained was a cloud of dust.

We stood in the pitch black of a warm Mexican night.

"Was that what they wanted?" I murmured. Gene reached my hands, pulled me to my feet, and hugged me.

In the silence, tears slipped down my cheeks. And then we filled the cooling night air with laughter.

"Don't worry, honey, I still have the pineapple."

# GARLIC—IT'S A SUPER HEALER

## LISA CHURCHVILLE

One of my earliest memories of my mom is her in a black leotard doing leg swings. She held the back of a dining chair and followed along with Jack LaLanne on our black-and-white television. Even though she made me finish all the vegetables on my plate and eat gag-inducing stewed prunes to keep me "regular," she also baked Toll House chocolate-chip cookies using the recipe from the back of the bag and always kept a box of Neapolitan ice cream in the freezer.

Then, in fifth grade, my parents divorced. While many people seem devastated when their parents split, that's not my memory. I just remember feeling relieved. Relieved and hopeful for no more turning up the radio in my room to drown out their fights; no more coming home from school and finding Mom locked in the bathroom, crying; and no more walking on eggshells, trying to decipher my father's mood after a few drinks.

Mom started dating a man who went from wheelchair to walking through juicing and good nutrition. Once we moved in with him, her health focus intensified. First, she replaced white bread with wheat, sugar with honey, and ice cream with frozen yogurt. While other kids brought Nature Valley granola bars in their lunches, I got Mom's homemade version—a stiff mud-looking concoction of carob, dates, nuts, and puffed rice.

In junior high, while other girls spent the weekend shopping or going out to lunch with their moms, mine preached the benefits of enemas. At that age, I didn't actively say *No*. I just ignored her, because even though I hated all the weird health crap, living with her and my stepdad in a calm, happy environment was a significant step up from her screaming fights with my father. I just went along to get along.

I survived on Campbell's soup and toast topped with that shitty peanut butter that had to be stirred and refrigerated. When my mom and stepdad installed a second refrigerator for the 100-pound bags of carrots they bought to juice, I exerted my independence with strategically planned visits to the neighbor's house right after school or around dinnertime. My friend James smiled the minute I entered his house, pointing to the pantry stocked with Chips Ahoy.

I spent the entire summer of 1987 counting down the days until I could run off to college for what I assumed would be the land of late-night pizza and new beginnings, finally living life on my terms. I worked as many shifts as possible at a clothing store at the mall so I could purchase cute bedding and dishes for my freshman dorm room at ASU. The rest of my time was spent at Canyon Lake perfecting my tan, so I'd look good in all the new clothes I bought with my discount.

But five days before my big move, I came home from a weekend sleepover with my legs and feet covered in flea bites. A major allergic reaction left me so itchy and swollen that I couldn't put on shoes.

I climbed into bed that night, and Mom brought me Benadryl and some calamine lotion. I swallowed the pills and carefully dabbed the cool liquid on each bite. By the time she turned out the lights, my pink leopard legs had calmed.

The relief didn't last, and I woke in the middle of the night with painful, bleeding legs. I didn't know what else to do, so I walked to Mom's door and lightly knocked.

In the bright light of the kitchen, she opened cupboard after cupboard, pondering and rejecting items that could be of use. I sat with my head on the table, trying to ignore the urge to poke at the painful spots until I heard her say, "Garlic. Raw garlic. That's a super healer."

I rolled my eyes. *Garlic, really?*

She reached over me to the basket of garlic my stepdad kept on the table.

"I'm super itchy. I think it's going to take more than choking down a bunch of garlic to stop this," I said.

"You're not going to eat it, honey. I'm going to make a poultice," she said, as she waltzed to the other side of the room.

"What's a poultice?"

"It's a paste of herbs a lot of people place on the bottom of their feet."

I grimaced. Before the internet, my mom got her health information from free pamphlets and books she'd pick up at the health food store.

"I'm thinking something like the mustard plaster people used as a home remedy for coughs and colds. I've never read about using garlic, but it's very healing, so why not try."

I shook my head from side to side, watching her excitement increase.

"We need to make a paste." She glanced at me. "How can I do that with raw garlic and make it stick?"

My gut screamed no, but I didn't say that. Instead, I offered up a meager objection. "This sounds weird. Don't we have any regular medicine that would work?"

"This is going to be great, honey. Don't you worry."

I was miserable, so I caved to this ridiculous idea.

She peeled the cloves and then whacked them into a pulp with a meat mallet. She decided Vaseline would do for the stickum part. She mixed them in a bowl, brought them to the table, carefully dabbed the thick concoction over each bite, and wrapped my legs like a mummy with cheesecloth.

It was about 2:00 a.m. by the time she walked me to bed. I crawled in, and she placed a couple of pillows under my legs to keep them elevated. As I drifted off, I noticed tiny warm tingling sensations, as if someone was holding a lit match under each bite. As the heat increased, I considered telling Mom something was wrong, but exhaustion won out, and I reassured myself instead that the garlic must be working.

I woke refreshed and grateful that Mom's weird remedy must've done the trick since I had no pain or itching. I needed to be at work in an hour, so I went straight to the bathroom to get cleaned up. I placed one foot on the side of the bathtub, unrolled the cheesecloth, and screamed. My leg was covered in dark-red puffy blisters. I unrolled the cloth from the other leg, and it was the same. The blisters were so full that they were hard to the touch. Mom came running in, took one look, and her hands went to her face.

"Oh no," she cried. "Something's gone terribly wrong!"

"You think?"

I was furious and scared. The beautiful, bronzed legs that I had planned to show off in my new shorts and miniskirts were covered in puffy sores. *What had she done to me?*

I called into work, and Mom called the doctor. We sat in the examination room, waiting, not speaking. I stared at a poster on the wall, stewing in anger. It seemed forever before the doctor pushed through the door with a smile.

"So, what brings you ladies in today?"

I waited for Mom to explain while the doctor looked patiently from one of us to the other. I didn't know what to say, so I stood up and lifted my long skirt.

His eyes widened. "Was there a grease fire?"

Mom and I turned toward each other and locked eyes. *How the hell do you explain this?* It started as nervous laughter, but then we couldn't stop.

"That looks like second-degree burns," the doctor said, as he glared at my mother.

*Second-degree burns?* That snapped us to attention, and laughter turned to tears.

I pointed at Mom with accusation. "She decided fresh garlic mixed with Vaseline was going to stop the itching I had from bug bites."

"Petroleum jelly and garlic?"

I nodded.

"Oh my," he said. "Second-degree burns are serious, and it's going to take a few months to heal. I'm hopeful the scars will fade within a year."

I looked at my legs and sobbed even harder. *This could be permanent?* At that moment, the doctor validated something deep inside of me that I already knew but hadn't acted on. Mom wasn't always right, and I didn't have to just go along with anything she said. In the car, she apologized over and over, but I was too mad to speak with her.

The worst part of moving to college was not being able to wear pants to cover my ugly legs. In the drying-out phase, the blisters wept as they started to heal. ASU was composed of 40,000 beautiful people, and I looked like a leper. My excitement to meet new friends came crashing down the first evening, while waiting for the dorm elevator to take me down to dinner. The doors opened, and the girls inside looked me over in my cute fluorescent-orange tank and miniskirt. Their eyes stopped and grew wide once they hit my thighs, then scanned down to my legs full of blisters. One gal quickly pressed the Door Close button as I approached.

Labor Day weekend, I went home for a quick visit. When packing my car to leave, Mom rushed out of the house with a bag full of healthy leftovers. I thought about taking the bag for a moment so I wouldn't upset her. But instead, I hugged her tight, looked her in the eye, and said, "No thanks."

# JUNGLED BUS STOP

MEGHAN CONLEY

"Come with us," Gabe said as he wiped the sweat off his brow. "Oliver and I head out tomorrow for Nicaragua. Can you change your plans?"

I was one month into my four-month trip through Costa Rica; I was traveling solo. And I liked it. I had never thought of traveling through all of Central America.

Meeting these very cute Canadians changed all that.

Gabe and Oliver were French Quebecers. While Oliver was tall with model good looks and adorable, it was Gabe that I connected with. He was smart, witty, and into books and philosophy. We talked for hours about travel, language, and how he was "all in favor of Quebec separating from Canada, so it becomes its own country." It didn't hurt that he looked just like Ralph Fiennes from *The English Patient*—handsome and rugged.

As a Minnesota girl, I was discovering a whole new world about my neighbors to the north. I wasn't expecting to meet potential boyfriend material, but it felt like Gabe and I had known each other for years instead of hours. The way we met was magical; it took me by surprise. It was nighttime, and Gabe and I had both been relaxing in the hot springs at La Fortuna when the nearby Arenal Volcano erupted. We watched in awe as it shot in the air and sent down rivers of burning red, yellow, and orange lava.

We soaked in the warm water and watched the liquid fire in the sky, mesmerized by nature's show. And we bonded. What were the odds to be there with him at that moment? Probably a billion to one.

The question lingered in the air. Did I want to go to Nicaragua with them?

It felt risky. And joining them meant scrapping all my plans. "I need more time to think about it."

"What about at least coming to join us in Liberia tomorrow? Our friend has a beautiful resort there."

So, I joined them on their next stop, Liberia in northern Costa Rica. Other than for the airport, no one really *goes* to Liberia—for anything. And surprise, they couldn't find their friend, and there was no resort, which is how we ended up camping on a deserted beach in Liberia, surrounded by the jungle.

The three of us huddled in a thin, small tent while Gabe flipped through his *Central America on a Shoestring* guidebook. As he read, I was getting hooked. Did I want to see six more countries? I looked at Gabe, and he looked at me, and there was a moment when I felt my entire body tingle.

"Yes, I'll go."

Gabe smiled.

"Only one problem," I said. I had left my passport back in San Jose, several hours away from Liberia by bus. "There's no way I can get my passport and leave with you guys in the morning," I said.

"We'll wait an extra day," Gabe said. My heart melted a little: *he'd wait for me.* Gabe looked through the guidebook. "So, it looks like you only have one shot of catching the only morning bus to San Jose. It leaves at 4:00 a.m."

I looked around at the deserted beach and then at the jungle. *But where exactly do I catch this bus?* Apparently, my only option would be to walk from our deserted beach through the jungle, probably full of spider monkeys, snakes, and wild boars, until I made it to the paved road and found the one streetlight—the bus stop—and wait.

By now, I had learned the Costa Rica bus rules: if the bus driver sees anyone there, the bus will stop. If no one is standing there, it will go on.

I must have been falling in love because I *am not* a morning person, and catching a bus before dawn sounded like torture. I cursed myself for having thought, *what a great idea, keep San Jose as a home base while traveling throughout Costa Rica.* Now, I had to take this four-hour bus ride, grab my passport and backpack, and take another four-hour bus ride back to reunite with Gabe and Oliver.

I left the campsite at 3:30 a.m. I looked around for a path, but it was pitch black. I felt more alone than I had ever been. It's one thing to walk by yourself in complete darkness; it's even more terrifying with jungle animals waiting in the wings to eat you for breakfast.

I jumped at every branch that snapped under my feet. As a breeze whipped by, I turned to see if I was being followed. The sounds of screeching, chirping, and howling seemed to grow louder with each step I took. I couldn't even see one foot in front of me as I slowly and cautiously shuffled down a nonexistent jungle path.

I didn't have a flashlight. There was no moonlight; darkness encircled me. Otherworldly sounds arose from every direction—up in the trees, behind the brush, right in front of me. My frantic thumping heartbeat merged with the intense "kah-kahs" and "woo-hoos" that seemed to be coming from unseen primates and exotic birds. Above me, I heard the howls of the screaming spider monkeys above my head, probably watching me and screeching, "Look at her! Should we attack?" I felt like Dorothy in the *Wizard of Oz,* walking the plank over the castle's moat where flying monkeys had trapped her.

Below me, I heard the crackling and crunching under my flip-flopped feet. With each step, I imagined treading on a poisonous snake or spider. After about fifteen minutes, I realized the fear was nearly paralyzing me. I felt feverish and drenched in sweat, the kind that pours out of your skin from pure adrenaline. I held my breath, trying not to make a sound.

*Stop walking. Turn back.*

It was then I felt a deep resolve wash over me. I was determined not to be that girl, the horror-movie-cliché girl who walks alone through the dark on a scary dirt road only to meet her demise.

If that bus exists, damn it, I'm going to make it.

I swallowed the lump in my throat, put one foot in front of the other, and chanted, "Just get to the road. Get to the light. Get on that bus." So, I pressed on.

Finally, I saw a small opening in the jungle path. *Sweet baby Jesus, it's the road.* I felt my legs moving faster, running toward the road and the streetlight in the distance. I exhaled. I made it out of that jungle.

Next, I ran to the streetlight, finding salvation in its warm glow. It was 3:50 a.m., and I was covered in sweat and still shaking with adrenaline. Then, it was 4:00 a.m., and I strained to hear the bus. Nothing. It was as silent as if time stood still in a black hole.

Then it was 4:10 a.m., and still no bus or signs of life on the street. I paced under the light. Two steps forward, two steps back. It was 4:15 a.m. A sick revelation came over me: the walk was all for nothing.

*Oh, my God. Gabe and Oliver had gotten it all wrong. There is no fucking 4:00 a.m. bus.*

This wasn't possible. I couldn't make that walk back to camp again in the dark. I had barely made it to the streetlight. I wanted to cry. I was about to have a full-blown nervous breakdown, knowing that my only option was to make that treacherous walk back to camp.

Five minutes later, like a miracle sent straight from heaven, a beacon of light came toward me. *Could it be the bus?* I waved my hands and stood on my tippy-toes, yelling to no one, "I'm here. I'm here! Please, stop. I'll die if you don't stop!"

The rickety old bus chugged closer, gas smell and all, and stopped. As I slowly climbed the steps onto the bus, my body released like a ragdoll. I beamed a smile full of relief and gratitude to the half-asleep driver who didn't even glance at me. And I silently made my way to the back of that glorious bus to San Jose.

It's been twenty-five years since that petrifying jungle walk. I have compassion for my twenty-two-year-old self, who was clueless but willing to brave whatever came my way, even if that meant walking through a dark jungle with deadly creatures, for a chance at love and travel. That lone walk led to a life where I have said yes to adventures more often than I have said no.

# WALKING THE BOULEVARD

NANCY MAE JOHNSON

Detective Gordon from the Sex Trafficking Unit of the San Diego Police Department rang into my classroom phone at Hoover High School.

"Do you want to interview one of the girls? I have a sex trafficking victim named Amy who testified in court. She wants to tell her story. She is pregnant by her pimp and has come in off the streets to get some help. If you pick a public spot downtown but private enough that you won't be on display, you should be all right."

I was not a journalist. I was a high school English teacher. But I was months away from retirement and was ready to try a new career.

I had met Detective Gordon a few weeks earlier at a fundraiser for STARS, a facility that helps young women escape their sex traffickers and return to a more healthy life. I had been invited to the event after attending a Parent Center information night at Hoover called "Protecting our Students from the Boulevard." I had taught there for over sixteen years and read thousands of journals from my immigrant students about abuse, incest, and violent relationships—but I'd never had a student share about being a victim of sex trafficking. Were my girls more vulnerable because they had already been sexually molested? I wanted to know.

I learned startling statistics on the day of the benefit. According to a January 2014 FBI report, a San Diego-based investigation recovered sixty female sex trafficking victims, including eleven minors. In its press release, the FBI reported that "twenty-four alleged North Park gang members [were] charged in an indictment . . . . The racketeering conspiracy involved cross-country sex trafficking of underage girls and women, plus murder, kidnapping, and robbery . . . ."

Detective Gordon shared about working undercover as a "john." Young girls were caught prostituting and later put in safe houses where they were protected and given life skills to change their destiny. Once they felt safe, their testimony was used to identify leaders of sex trafficking rings across the United States.

"Do you think any of my students might be involved with sex trafficking or pimping?" I asked Detective Gordon.

"Absolutely. Many Hoover students have been propositioned, threatened, or are already working the streets."

For every story I shared with the detective, he had hundreds of similar stories.

"I'd like to learn more to give my students information that will keep them safe. When I retire, I want to compile a book full of journal entries and interviews with students of all cultures and backgrounds to help young women navigate their teenage years."

"Let me make a phone call. I have someone in mind."

I had asked him why our students become prostitutes and learned that every year, hundreds of San Diego girls who may have started out being abused in their homes, by their boyfriends, or simply by a stranger at a party, become victims of sex trafficking. We don't want to understand that victims of sexual abuse may continue to be sexually abused if they are manipulated with promises of love, money, and possibility. I had to give up my archaic understanding that those involved in sex crimes were involved by their own choice.

On our appointed interview day, as I fought to keep my stomach from flipping like the fish on the restaurant sign above my head, my mind flashed back to Ella, a student who had written about her fear when her mother left for work each night. Mom worked at the twenty-four-hour Mexican restaurant on Twenty-Second and University Avenue from 6:00 p.m. to 2:00 a.m. Her father drank his first Taurino Cerveza when he walked in the door after working all day, shoveling someone else's dirt or loading someone else's discarded couches, chairs, or broken appliances. Their rejects kept him comfortable while he made his way through a twelve-pack before the evening was done. The light would creep into this young girl's room when the door to her bedroom was pushed ajar. She would pray and feign sleep. But it didn't matter what she said to God or what she did to try and fool her drunken father; he would overpower her delicate body time and time again.

I had asked her to stay after class the next day and disclosed my obligation to Child Protective Services and what it meant to be a mandated reporter. More importantly, I shared my concern for her safety and well-being. She screamed, "You have no business ruining my life! You have no idea what will happen to me!" She cried and pleaded with me not to tell.

\*\*\*

I returned to the reality in front of me. I stood up and flagged down a young woman who matched the description given to me by Detective Gordon. Amy sat across from me at The Tin Fish restaurant, which was within walking distance of Father Joe's Village, where she was living. The patrons lucky enough to be enjoying the beautiful weekday morning would never know that eight months ago, Amy's testimony had helped in the arrest of four major players in a San Diego sex trafficking ring. We settled on a table removed from the fray, and Amy nonchalantly but incessantly scanned her environment. Amy had stunning, piercing, golden eyes. She was visibly pregnant, wearing blue jeans and a yellow V-neck top that showed a tattoo across her chest. Down her arms, there were three other small tattoos, the last right above her wrist where mangled scars were visible. Her short brown hair was covered with a blue and purple scarf pulled over her forehead and tied in the back. From her backpack, she brought out a small recorder. She asked if she could play a poem she wrote while in jail.

*Fuck the world in which I live.*
*I'm tired of being pushed, shoved,*
*abused and used after all that I give.*
*These men are scoundrels, piss ants,*
*and poor hustlin' asshole fools.*

*I won't take their mistreatment or bull.*
*As a prostitute, call girl, drug dealer, student,*
*I don't have time to be played like a fool.*
*That's why I started way back when I was just ten years old,*
*using my body, not as a treasure, but as a tool*
*to get around all the dumb ass male fools.*
*And I'll die living by that rule.*

**[The poem and our conversation transcript are reprinted here with her permission.]**

**Nancy:** What has it been like for you since that poem was written?

**Amy:** It's kind of weird staying in a homeless shelter, but I want to create a life for my baby. I never know whether someone is going to come try to take her or whether somebody is going to shoot me or kill me once the baby is born. I've had this pimp's family chase me around town saying, "Oh, wait until that baby's born. I'm going to kill you, shoot you dead. She'll live on without you."

**Nancy:** That's terrifying.

**Amy:** And if it weren't for me being able to call the detective and the girls from BSCC [Bilateral Safety Corridor Coalition], I wouldn't know who to turn to, you know? Other than God.

What they do is they bust us working girls, us escorts. They send an undercover officer to our room to get us. Once they have us in custody, then they interrogate us until they break us down—and it's not hard to break us down, although it took them thirteen and a half hours to get me to break.

While I was waiting in a hotel, I broke off a piece of glass from the mirror in my room and slit my wrists because I knew my pimp would find me either before or after the trial and kill me anyway. The blood scared me, and I called one of the detectives who had given me his card. He sent an ambulance and transferred me to a safe house until trial.

**Nancy:** Can you go way back to your earliest memory of family or street life?

**Amy:** I was taken from my mother when I was nine; she was a crack-addicted prostitute. Her drugs meant more to her than I did.

Men meant more to her than I did. So, I became a runaway, fleeing from twenty-nine foster homes and sixteen group homes. By the time I was fifteen, I was facing incarceration in an adult prison for sex trafficking charges for my oldest son's father, my son who is now nineteen.

I got pregnant when I was ten. My mom offered my body as payment for a $10 piece of rock cocaine. I had my son at eleven.

**Nancy:** Were you in a foster home at that time?

**Amy:** No. I ran away and lived with the baby's father, the drug dealer. I was gone the entire time that I was pregnant that time. I didn't go to prenatal care, and I was locked in a room by myself. Every time I tried to go outside, he would block me. I had home delivery.

Even before I got pregnant, I started snorting cocaine when I was ten years old. By the time I was fourteen, I was using crack, smoking pot, drinking, hanging out late at night. I started tricking out my body when I was thirteen, mostly to my mom's tricks or johns.

***

Amy at thirteen could have been my student. Would she have written about these horrific experiences in her journal? Would I have been able to help?

Teachers never know what happens after we file Child Protective Services reports, and a student will rarely give up the details to an informant. Ella, the student who wrote about abuse by her father, stopped talking to me after my CPS report. She didn't make it through the school year. A year later, she showed up in my classroom after school one day. The second I made eye contact with her, she began to cry. Ella walked across the room into my arms, and by the time she reached me, I was crying too. She said, "You saved my life. I just wanted you to know."

# FIFTEEN MINUTES OF FORTUNE

## HAYLI NICOLE

I jumbled the oversized dice in my trembling hands, expelling air from my blowfish cheeks as if that would somehow bring more luck. The dice tumbled down the carpeted ramp, but I didn't see their final resting place. My eyes were closed tight, and both hands were twisted into a lucky cross of the fingers. How did I come to be dressed as an elf, rolling dice against a lanky gentleman named Nicolas wearing too-short gym shorts and an afro wig with Wayne Brady standing between us?

Eight months prior, I was a mess of a human, feeling doomed to a Groundhog Day existence. My parents had used my student loan money to fix up the house, which eventually foreclosed and forced me to drop out of college. My father had left our family for his mistress and their secret love child. My extended family still lived in the same neighborhood where Nana raised them. I had given up on the hopes of getting out of San Diego and doing something more with my life.

Until the morning of April 18, 2012.

I woke up gasping for air, as if an elephant was crushing my chest. I inhaled sharply, and my torso went into spasms. Kaiser admitted me to the emergency room with severe chest pain, but for seven hours, doctors told me it was probably just gas, and nurses accused me of being admitted for attention.

Something called a D-dimer, which indicated blood clots, came back positive on my tests. The doctor assured me it was a false positive, since I was a healthy twenty-two-year-old. However, he ordered a CT scan to be sure. Not only did the results come back that I had blood clots, but apparently, I had suffered from a pulmonary embolism triggered by birth control, and I needed to be admitted to the hospital immediately. In a single moment, my world as a healthy young woman imploded. Behind the curtain, I heard the nurse and the physician's assistant arguing.

"Why wasn't this the first thing tested?"

"She presented normally. Her O2 saturation was in the high 80s. She's so young."

"You realize this would have killed her, don't you?"

Despite being admitted for a few days, the severity of the near-death incident wouldn't hit me until several months later. My veins collapsed from daily blood draws. Yoga left me covered in painful bruises, so I abandoned exercise altogether. The warfarin triggered blackouts.

After one outpatient visit where my INR levels, which measure the time it takes for the blood to clot, were triple the normal range and threatened another hospitalization, I sat in my car sobbing. *This isn't how a twenty-two-year-old should live!* I drove home and happened upon a bucket list I wrote when my full-time profession was adolescent daydreaming. What were some things I wanted to do with my life? As a seventeen-year-old, I wanted to jump out of an airplane, perform standup comedy at an open mic, publish a book, ride a motorbike through Vietnam, and maybe go to Germany? Taking inventory of the nothingness of the last five years, I asked myself, what is the point of a second chance at life if I am too fragile to live?

I weighed three major scenarios and the risks—remaining on warfarin for the rest of my life and bleeding out internally if I sustained any injury, the fatal potential of another blood clot if I remained on birth control, or ridding my body of all medication against every doctor's advice in an attempt to take back my life.

Without hesitation, I chose life and all of the risks that came with it.

I immediately stopped taking the warfarin. I went off birth control. I started physical therapy to build strength in my muscles. Then, I went after the bucket-turned-life list. In rapid succession, I became the Yes Woman. I jumped out of the airplane. I rode in a hot air balloon. I started performing standup comedy. I even got a job as a karaoke host despite being unable to carry a tune myself.

On December 15, a veteran comedian named Guam Felix posted in our local comedy group on Facebook: "I need eight comics that want to be on *Let's Make a Deal* in Hollywood. You have to have a costume and love to dance and be crazy. It's the most fun show ever."

I had never heard of the show before, but over a dozen comedians responded to Guam's call to action. With zero inhibitions, I drove to LA at 4:00 a.m. four days later to join a few local comedians and a man I knew from the internet. In a scramble that morning, I pulled on bright green leggings and a green tunic from a Peter Pan costume. I found a Christmas hat with elf ears glued on that I think my mom bought at a gas station.

I stood on the corner of Sunset and Van Ness dressed as an elf. A homeless man was pissing on the brick wall next to me, and I had to remind myself I was the spectacle. I questioned my clearheadedness and my safety. Suddenly, I saw this jolly Asian man dressed as a court jester and waving in my direction. Guam's bear hug and joyous energy flooded me with relief.

The line for ticket holders wrapped around the gates of Sunset Bronson Studios. As we walked to the end of the line, my cheeks felt flush seeing a few Santas and ten other elves standing in line. *Come to a Christmas taping dressed as an elf. Nailed it.*

"So, how many other comedians are coming?"

"Oh, you're the only person who followed through," Guam stated casually.

Which meant Guam and I were in this together, two freezing-cold strangers in a line of costume-clad contestants hoping for their fifteen minutes of fortune.

We checked in with the studio staff, were provided a number and a name tag, and were corralled into a room with empty chairs. Show producers sat at the front with their backs to us, interviewing groups of contestants. I was too overwhelmed to be enthusiastic. A woman dressed as a giant stack of Christmas presents spoke to a guy in a gorilla suit. A hula dancer stood next to a caveman. I think I saw a Dalmatian do a cartwheel. There was most definitely a giant chicken.

Once we entered the studio, we found ourselves in a sea of dancing, flailing, costumed bodies. This is the part I didn't expect. Those commercial breaks are wild dance parties. The producers watch from mirrored windows to select their desired contestants. Guam and I were having a blast banging our bodies to '80s classics, but my injured lungs reminded me I should probably pace myself. The producers didn't pick us for the first taping, but a stage assistant stopped us as we exited the studio.

"Any chance you want to stay for the afternoon taping? It will increase your chances of getting picked, and we'll seat you somewhere central!" Guam and I quickly conferred and accepted. As promised, we were seated center stage. When a new contestant is selected for a segment on *Let's Make a Deal*, they are either called by name because Big Brother has been watching them sweat their ass off for two hours, or they get the attention of the host, Sir Wayne Brady, and he calls them by costume.

Contestants are discouraged from jumping and shouting during taping, so I imagined myself ten feet taller than everyone else in the room. Wayne entered the crowd, and I did everything possible to get his attention. Just as he was about to point to a man in a toga, we locked eyes across the room. His finger whipped in my direction and he said, "Elf, come with me." I sprinted to the stage. It was utter Christmas magic.

Nicolas's and my game was the Dice Duel. The numbers two to twelve on the die reveal a dollar amount added to your bank. If you roll a number twice, the game is over. You can trade in a Free Roll card for another toss of the dice. Simple enough.

The segment should have gone quickly, but we gave the audience a proper showdown. With each successful roll, our heart rates doubled, and our banks increased. After a bunk roll, Wayne proposed an offer. "You could give that Free Roll card back to me, or I could just give you $300 to quit. One of you is going home with nothing." I pretended to be in a conundrum but shouted, "I'm going to keep playing!"

By the look on his face, I think Wayne Brady was just as shocked to see me roll that ten as I was. With $1300 added to my bank, my broke-ass college student mind couldn't comprehend the possibility of going home with $4600. All that remained in the duel were two, four, eight, and twelve.

Nicolas rolled another nine, rejected Wayne's offer to forfeit the game, and used his Free Roll card instead. He wasn't going down without a fight; my financial fate was in his hands. I crossed my fingers again and blocked my eyes. Nicolas rolled another three, putting an end to our dice duel.

Suddenly, I let out the sincerest scream I didn't even know was in my register. We cut to a commercial break, and as soon as I sat down, all the color drained from my face. I don't remember anything else from the taping. All I could think about was which debt I should pay off first. I was escorted to a shaggy office to sign an NDA. You're not allowed to tell a single person about the show's results until it airs, and you must wait six weeks to receive your prize. Guam and I stopped somewhere for a burrito and checked my bank account's balance. I had sixty-two dollars to my name. I was both the poorest and the wealthiest I had ever been.

When I returned to San Diego the next day, I asked my best friend Jimmy, who always supported my wild ideas, how he felt about me leaving for a while to travel.

Unfazed, he asked, "Where would you go?"

"I think I'll go to Germany."

# MY DAY WITH A HOMELESS CRIMINAL

LIBBY KNAPP

He was scrappy, clad in shorts and a ski jacket. His curly black hair fell around his tattooed face and neck. He carried a tattered bag and a case of water. He slumped, walking with an air of defeat. Hopelessness. A commanding sheriff almost twice his size with a beer gut towered over him. I had been driving by, having just left the small airport in a town on the northern coast of California. I could have kept driving home. But then a moment flashed through my mind: the time when my son was alone in Nicaragua and was mugged. I had always wished someone would have helped him.

I felt compelled, directed, to pull over to the curb. As I reached the homeless man and the sheriff, I rolled down the window. "Is everything okay?"

"Yes, ma'am, we are fine," the sheriff tossed off, thinking I would drive away. But I stayed. The sheriff stepped off the curb and leaned into my window.

"Do you think it would be okay if I gave him a ride to the closest bus station?" I knew the Greyhound bus station was about seven miles away down Highway 101.

The imposing sheriff offered me an "are you crazy" look. "That is up to you, ma'am."

I called out to the homeless man. As he walked closer, I could see the item in his hands. A large black trash bag, the kind that people use to collect the leaves on their lawn. I saw that he had two teardrop tattoos under his left eye. Tattoos covered his neck. I reached across and opened the passenger door and waved him in. He cautiously placed his meager belongings in the back seat and sat in my passenger seat. We pulled out. I felt like my brain was moving in slow motion. No words passed between us as we drove out of the airport. I glanced over and noticed he wore white high-top tennis shoes that looked almost new, with clean white socks.

About five minutes into the drive, I asked him, "What's your name?"

He looked at his shoes and mumbled, "Well, I guess you can call me Jason."

My next question was, "How in the world did you end up sleeping out here in the middle of nowhere on a tiny bench in front of an airport?"

Jason mumbled again. I could not understand him. He lifted his chin a little and spoke up. "I got out of Pelican Bay eight days ago."

I felt a small twitch of fear in my gut. "What is Pelican Bay?"

With a hint of shock, he said, "It's a prison north of here about seventy-five miles. I just got paroled after two years for good behavior."

I calculated that we were halfway to the bus station by this time and close to an off-ramp with a hotel and a gas station. The logical part of my brain screamed, *get off the road, get him out of your car; what are you doing?* And then I felt a calm sense of guidance, almost as if an angel was behind me. I kept driving.

"What were you in for?" I asked, hoping it was not for something violent.

Jason explained that he had been sentenced to three years for breaking and entering a business to steal for drugs. He had been in a program in Los Angeles called Homeboy Industries that helped gang members get out of "the life." He was working there, getting sober, but he lost it one night—a relapse that landed him in prison.

We sat in the car for a moment when we arrived at the bus station. I asked him if there was anyone that he could call back home. "Homeboy Industries, I have a number I memorized."

I handed him my phone. He spoke to a man named Hector, whom he had worked with before he got arrested. "Hey, Hector, I just got out, and I'm coming to LA."

Next, we called Jason's aunt. Within a few moments, I could hear her yelling at him for being a "fucking idiot." I asked for the phone. Hurt, frustration, and fury dripped in her every word as she told me not to trust him, to realize he was a drug addict who could not control his own actions.

"Thank you for the information," I said. Thoughts flooded my mind. *Should I just say good luck and make him get out of the car? Should I buy him a ticket? Is he on drugs right now?*

Some part of me wondered: why am I even doing this? And another part of me knew exactly why. It was about my mom. When I was thirteen, my mom committed suicide. We had been fighting for over a year. I blamed her for my father leaving us. She would throw chairs and ashtrays at me, and I would tell her I hated her and wished she wasn't my mom. I would often run to the beach and scream at the ocean at the top of my lungs.

At eighteen, with my first husband, I began my lifelong dance as a rescuer. I could sense a person in trouble, and a primal urge would pull me toward them. In therapy, I learned that I was processing the guilt for not being able to save my mom. And here I was doing it again.

I looked at Jason. Despair swirled around him. He was afraid to look at me—afraid I might see something that would make me run away. Yet, I knew I would help him one way or the other.

We entered the smallest bus station I have ever seen. The one employee was a stern-looking woman with black horn-rimmed glasses and salt-and-pepper hair. The first thing she said to us was, "Hey, I've seen you before. What are you doing back in here?"

My new friend shrugged his shoulders. "I went to Eureka for a few days with a friend. We tried mining, and I saw a castle."

Sarcasm dripped. "Ya, right, and I suppose you spent all of your probation check, right"?

Jason mumbled under his breath, "Yes, ma'am."

I spoke up and explained to her that I had just picked him up at the Eureka-Arcata Airport, and we were interested in how much a ticket to Los Angeles would cost. She, too, looked at me like I was crazy and said it was $150 and that the next bus left at 9:45 a.m. the next morning. I bought the ticket, and we made our way back to the car.

I pulled out my cell phone and looked up homeless shelters. The closest one was in Eureka, which is well known in the county for being heaven for meth users. That did not feel safe for Jason. Then, what popped up on my phone was that a homeless shelter was actually right next door.

Again, I had that feeling that something or someone was guiding us. We gathered Jason's belongings and walked over to the small shelter.

At the entrance, we took in the sight of twenty or so homeless people in a line to get in—all carrying their worldly belongings in bags or carts—all wondering what was next. Anxiety. Drug use. Despair.

When we made it to the front of the line, the manager said he would hold Jason's bus ticket until the next morning.

For a moment, I thought of leaving Jason there and then. But I could see the look in the eyes of the drug users that surrounded us. And I knew that if I left now, Jason would not make it on that bus.

It suddenly dawned on me that I was starving.

"Are you hungry?"

We headed to downtown Arcata just a couple of blocks away and found the Arcata Co-op store. As we shopped for cheese and crackers and chips and salsa, I found myself sharing my own personal recovery story. I told this stranger about my mom. He listened intently.

"My mom died of a drug overdose when I was seventeen," he said. He told me that he had a family: an ex-wife, and two daughters he had not spoken to in over ten years. "They kicked me out when I was doing drugs. I don't think they will ever forgive me."

As we purchased the groceries and found a small deli inside the market, I shared with him that my dad and stepmom were self-centered and pretty lousy parents, but I had been able to forgive them.

"Your daughters will forgive you if you reach out," I said. He shrugged his shoulders.

After lunch, I dropped him off at the homeless shelter. I looked him in the eyes. "We will meet here at 9:00 a.m. tomorrow, right?"

"Right."

The next morning, I drove up and Jason was standing there, large black bag in hand, ready to get on the bus. Something had shifted; he almost looked excited about the journey. He told me he had spent the night behind a bush in front of the homeless shelter and had not bought drugs. Relief washed through me. It was then that I saw a wave of emotion engulf him.

"Thank you. Thank you. Thank you," he repeated, as we walked toward the bus. He asked if he could give me a hug.

"Yes," I said. As we hugged, I whispered, "Thank you for letting me help you."

# STRENGTH TRAINING

KENNY SUCHER

"Something funny, gentlemen?" said Coach Brock, projecting his voice to the entire class. Three ropes hung threateningly behind him. His camouflage-colored Nike shirt was wrapped around his muscular torso like cellophane. He had just demonstrated how to climb the rope, grasping it with his hands, lassoing his feet, then using the strength from his tree-trunk-sized thighs to push himself up. My friend had whispered jokingly, "Bad time to be camouflaging your body; where is he?" It wasn't funny, but I'd laughed anyway, more from nervousness that I'd be asked to do this soon.

Coach Brock continued, "If you think it's so funny, you must already know how to climb these ropes."

We shook our heads with widening eyes, attempting to convey that we had no idea what we were doing. This was the first time they'd asked me to climb a rope in CrossFit, but those ropes had been dangling there ominously since my first day over a year ago. I was quickly approaching my forties, and I had decided I wanted to not only look strong; I wanted to *be* strong. I had researched CrossFit gyms in my area, quickly learning they don't call them *gyms*. They call them *boxes*.

The box I chose was in a large warehouse-sized room that smelled of sweat and chalk, with a faint aroma of burnt skin. I decided to go to a beginner's demo class, where we used a PVC pipe to mimic core CrossFit movements. After the supposedly free demo, I suddenly found myself signing a contract and handing over my credit card for the $165 monthly fee. This was a "friends and family" rate, I was told by the muscular head coach with piercing green eyes and a chiseled jawline. He kept casually pulling his shirt up to wipe his mouth, exposing his taut abs as he swindled me. It was like I was back in elementary school, and the bully was taking my lunch money. And just like those bullies, there was a smarmy charm about him that was both threatening and arousing.

The actual class involved real weights, which were stacked up like poker chips in the corner. The workout of the day, or WOD, was written on a large whiteboard next to a hall of famer list highlighting the best times for various popular WODs like the *Cindy* and the *Helen*. Someone once asked a coach why so many popular CrossFit workouts were named after women. "Because they're a bitch," he said.

The WOD for my first real day of CrossFit was named *Fran*. After our warm-up run, Coach Dave demoed the workout. It was a relatively simple routine involving repeated sets of thrusters and pullups. A thruster, he showed us, was basically squatting with the barbell and thrusting it into the air upon standing, like evangelicals at a raucous revival. Twenty-one thrusters and pullups, then fifteen, then nine, until you finish or collapse from exhaustion, overcome by the Spirit.

The classes took place in a cavernous room lined with all the necessary equipment. Except for mirrors. No mirrors in sight. As the head coach had explained during my introductory demo, while again nonchalantly lifting his shirt up, this was a vanity-free zone.

I missed mirrors while I was at CrossFit, although it was mirrors that I avoided when I first started going to the gym back in my twenties. Around that same time, not coincidentally, I came out of the closet. I had a foot out for a while, but when I was twenty-four years old, I flung the door open and sashayed out, ready for whatever might come my way—which ended up being rejection. Lots of it. I had never had a problem with women. They'd usually get so attached I had to reject them. I realize now that part of their attraction to me was probably due to the indifference I gave off. Like a pheromone. I wished I could have bottled that.

Instead of giving off the feeling of indifference to men, I served desperation. Ladles full of it. I broke all the rules. I'd call them the next day. Or the same day. Or even moments after they left. I even called a guy once at his job, a large sporting goods store he mentioned working at, asking if he had missed all my other calls.

"I've been busy," he said. But it sounded more like a question or a plea from a hostage. I seemed to lack an ability to detect their disinterest in me, a disinterest that was at least partly due to my over interest in them. I had just missed out on so many years of dating men, that I wanted to jump right in.

Instead of realizing that I was coming on too strong, I decided that any rejection was caused by me being out of shape. I had been skinny all my life but started gaining some weight in grad school. This was most likely due to the stress of classes and the sudden change in my metabolism. But being gay and out of shape was just code for *undesirable*. Or at least so I thought. I liked myself fine in clothes but less so out of them. So, I decided I was secretly fat. And I assumed men just ran once they discovered that secret.

I started cutting out foods like pasta, candy, and my daily intake of pizza. And it didn't take long for the fat to simply melt away. I started receiving compliments about my new physique and disbelief at how quickly it had happened. Luckily, I was a naturally thin person who just needed a slight diet adjustment. I worried, though, that my luck would run out soon. I started a stricter diet, and the gym became a daily ritual for me. Like the pizza used to be.

At first, this all felt great; I was happy with the transition my body had made. But soon, I started comparing myself to the guys in the gym with better physiques. I became frustrated that my legs were too skinny, and my abs weren't defined enough. And I soon felt out of shape again. Still secretly fat. Secretly flawed.

I wasn't alone in feeling this, although it felt like it most of the time. It's a story that's true for many gay men, which is why the gym is packed with us. Lifting, running, sweating away the shame. Most of the DC gays went to a gym called Vida. It was essentially a bar, with weights instead of booze; it even had a DJ some days. It was fun for a while, but I started to feel that my weight-training routine was superficial, because of course it was, and I decided to focus on gaining real strength.

I'm still not sure why I thought I needed to be any stronger. It was like I happened upon a fork in the road of middle age, and instead of choosing a path to the left or right, I flipped over the gigantic tractor tire separating the two. But joining a CrossFit gym—excuse me, *box*—requires a leap of faith, and like most faiths, you're not really supposed to question it; just accept your calling and jump.

Or thrust, in the case of that first day of rope training. Coach Dave asked us to demo the exercise for him. He didn't like my form, and his corrections weren't helping. "Ugh, I hate training Vida boys," he said. It brought me back to fourth grade and my PE coach, a probable former schoolyard bully, who always seemed personally offended that I could never make a layup shot. "You missed again, Tinkerbell," he'd say.

Weight suggestions were written below the WOD routine. Ninety-five pounds for men, sixty-five for women. Twenty-one reps of anything seemed excessive to me. I glanced around the room to glean what others were doing. I saw a guy grab two fifteen-pound weights. I decided to go slightly lower, grabbing two large rubber-coated ten-pound weights to add to my forty-five-pound bar. Nearby, a woman who looked near the end of her second trimester grabbed two fifteen-pound weights. I immediately switched mine out for the heavier ones.

The workout started, and I labored through, squatting and thrusting into the air. I'd mentally skip ahead in the rep counts so I wouldn't fall too far behind. But as the end of the hour grew near, I wasn't even close to finished. I saw others reracking their weights. The pregnant woman was finished too. They all started to gather around me. Watching. Leering. The intent was encouragement, but it felt menacing. "CrossFit is a family, and we don't leave our family members behind," I heard someone say. I wondered if Charles Manson ever gave a similar speech. I skipped a few more rep counts and finally finished, collapsing in exhaustion. The pregnant woman started carrying my weights back for me.

As I walked out, Coach Dave gave me a high five. "How was it?" he asked.

"Hard," I said.

"Do you feel like throwing up? You know you tried hard enough if you throw up," he said, adding, "You're one of the lucky ones. At least you look like you're in shape."

It's probably that last comment that made me come back. Like he saw me for the fraud I was. I wasn't tough, I wasn't strong, but I wanted to look *and be* in shape. So, I persisted.

I started to attend regularly. Calluses grew on my hands, like small badges of honor. I got better but not great at the myriad of CrossFit exercises. I even started finding myself attracted to the hot straight guys, since there were slim gay pickings at this box. It was like being in prison. And near the end, I was just looking for a way out.

\*\*\*

"Well, gentlemen. The class is waiting. Which one of you experts is going to demonstrate rope climbing for the class, since you found my demo so fucking funny?" Coach Brock said.

My friend's eyes darted to the ground. His lips pursed. His jaw clenched. My shoulders straightened, and my chest swelled. I took a deep breath, summoning all the courage I could, and said aloud, "Neither of us is doing anything. And if you ask again, I will leave." I was finally echoing the words I'd always imagined myself saying to that fourth-grade asshole PE teacher. And my dad. And all the other bullies I'd acquiesced to in my life.

"And I don't appreciate you talking to me this way. We are paying for this class," I added, now echoing the words of my mother's typical conversations with customer service representatives.

The coach's shoulders slumped forward, and his posture and voice softened. "Please, let's talk about this in the corner," he said.

We moved just a few feet away from the assembled class, who craned their necks in our direction as we spoke in enunciated whispers.

"Bro, sorry about that. I was just trying to motivate you," he said.

"Well, that method isn't going to be very effective on me."

After a few more awkward exchanges, we returned to the group. I was smiling. He wasn't. But he had apologized, and it felt good. Like breaking a horse. I assume. I mean, he was a stud.

I continued with the class that day. I even eventually made it halfway up the rope. And I came back a handful of times to CrossFit over the next few weeks. I even saw Coach Brock again. He walked up to me and smiled. Like we were old friends. A stallion to a gelding. I quit CrossFit soon after and returned to superficial muscles and smooth hands. But I knew I was quitting not because any coach scared me off but because I'd proved to myself that I'd found my real strength.

# ABOUT THE EDITORS

## MARNI FREEDMAN

**Marni Freedman** is a screenwriter, playwright, award-winning author, writing coach, and co-founder and director of programming for the San Diego Writers Festival. Marni leads the Memoir Certificate Program for San Diego Writers, Ink, is the executive producer of the International Memoir Writers Association's theatrical Memoir Showcase, and co-edits Shaking the Tree: brazen. short. memoir. You can find Marni at MarniFreedman.com, a hub to help writers find their authentic voice.

## TRACY J. JONES

**Tracy J. Jones** is a professional content writer, editor, and writing coach. She co-produces the International Memoir Writers Association's theatrical Memoir Showcase and is an editor of the Showcase anthology, Shaking the Tree: brazen. short. memoir. Tracy runs several read-and-critique groups, teaches at San Diego Writers, Ink, and is the interviewer for the Warwick's + San Diego Writers Festival Book Club. She's a freelance editor for Acorn Publications. She can be reached at tjjones1@gmail.com.

# SPECIAL THANKS

Jeniffer Thompson and her team at Monkey C Media for our beautiful cover and overall design. Erin Willard for copy-editing the manuscript. Anastasia Hipkins for proofreading the manuscript. The entire International Memoir Writers Association for supporting this project, as well as the San Diego Writers Festival. The IMWA Board: Marni Freedman, Laura L. Engel, Chloe Sparacino, Tracy J. Jones, Jeniffer Thompson, Caroline Gilman, M. Annette Ketner, Janet Hafner, John Cunningham, and Leslie Ferguson. And additional thanks to all our donors and angel supporters who have allowed these stories to be shared with our larger memoir community.

# ARE YOU A MEMOIRIST?

The International Memoir Writers Association is a community of writers committed to the art and craft of memoir writing. Our purpose is to create a community of inspired, informed, and nurtured memoirists. We host monthly member meetings with speakers who educate our writers in both the craft and business of memoir writing, present an annual Memoir Showcase where five-page pieces are professionally performed on stage, and support the San Diego Writers Festival. Writers of all levels and from all locations are welcome and encouraged to join us to help build their own writing community.

### Follow Us!

InternationalMemoirWriters.org
Facebook: www.facebook.com/groups/sdmemoirwriters
Twitter: @SD_MWA
Instagram: @sdmwa

Also check out:
SanDiegoWritersFestival.com

**Winner of the 13th Annual
National Indie Excellence Award
for an Anthology**

# *Shaking the Tree: brazen. short. memoir.*
## *(Volume 1)*

The Memoir Showcase is proud to present a selection of our most compelling true stories, drawn from our annual content. These pivotal portraits speak to our diverse community and its willingness to share the most challenging, awe-inspiring moments that make up the human experience. From a life-changing moment with a Maasai warrior to a wild and unexpected coming-of-age tale in a carnival, *Shaking the Tree* reveals moments of courage, humor, and vulnerability. The stories within these pages are breathtaking.

You can't make this stuff up.

## CONTRIBUTORS:

Mahshid Fashandi Hager
Anastasia Zadeik
John Cunningham
Judy Reeves
Kelly Hudson
Shawna Rawlinson
Elizabeth Oppen Eshoo
Cherie Kephart
Laura L. Engel
Barbara Huntington
Natalie Freedman
Donna Jose
Kathleen Holstad Pease
KM McNeel
Richard Farrell

Philip Pressel
Marijke McCandless
Sara Mohtashamipour
Ruth Laugesen
Danielle B. Baldwin
Leslie Johansen Nack
Catherine Spearnak
Steve Montgomery
Sarah Vosburgh
Ilene Hubbs
Kristen Balelo
Nancy G. Villalobos
Dilia Wood
Tracy J. Jones

Available at amazon.com, barnesandnoble.com, and indiebound.org.

# Shaking the Tree: brazen. short. memoir. (Volume 2)

The San Diego Memoir Writers Association is honored to present the second volume of compelling true stories drawn from our annual Memoir Showcase contest. This year's winning selections addressed the theme of "Things We Don't Talk About," and our writers bravely answered the call to share the most intimate narratives of their lives.

The authors take on bold issues such as hidden racism, physical and sexual abuse, illicit affairs, the tragic loss of a child or parent, secret family members, and the painfully awkward experiences of adolescent first love. Sometimes hilarious, sometimes terrifying or mysterious, the stories within these pages challenge us to check our assumptions, seek out understanding, and connect with the triumphant bravery it takes to shine a light on our secrets.

You can't make this stuff up.

## CONTRIBUTORS:

Elise Kim Prosser PhD
Krisa Bruemmer
Huda Al-Marashi
Laura L. Engel
Lauren Halsted
CJ Elliott
Lenore Greiner
Donna L. Jose
James Roberts
Bill Peters
Nancy "Pants" Johnson
Kimberly Joy
Misha Luz
Amanda Byzak
Katya McLane
Patricia Geist-Martin

Lynn Gahman
Marilyn Woods
Janice Alper
Marijke McCandless
Heather M. Berberet
Sarah Vosburgh
Laura May
Susan F. Keith
Caroline Gilman
Saadia Ali Esmail
MarDestinee C. Perez
John Cunningham
Laura Jaye
Madonna Treadway
Melissa Bloom

Available at amazon.com, barnesandnoble.com,
and indiebound.org.

# Shaking the Tree: brazen. short. memoir. (Volume 3)

The International Memoir Writers Association is honored to present the third volume of compelling true stories drawn from our annual Memoir Showcase contest. This year's winning selections address the theme of I Didn't See That One Coming. While these stories were written before the global pandemic, they offer reflections on how unseen events shape our lives.

This bold and entertaining volume is filled with riveting stories, such as being kidnapped at gunpoint and solving the mystery of the father you never knew, as well as lighthearted pieces about having the best sex of your life in your eighties. In the spirit of the Shaking the Tree series, this book goes there—unapologetically.

You can't make this stuff up.

## CONTRIBUTORS:

Elise Kim Prosser, PhD
Chili Cilch
Krisa Bruemmer
Kenny Sucher
Laura L. Engel
Elizabeth Eshoo
Nicola Ranson
Judy Reeves
Diane L. Schneider, MD
Tina Martin
Sandi Nieto
Cindy Jenson-Elliott
Nicole Gibbs
James Roberts
Vincentia Schroeter

Kimberly Joy
Nancy Mae Johnson
Tania Pryputniewicz
Lauren Halsted
Deborah Rudell
Jennifer Gasner
Anastasia Zadeik
Marijke McCandless
Nancy G. Villalobos
Heather M. Berberet
Chloe Sparacino
Sarah Vosburgh
Allan E. Musterer
Eileen Mathena
Suzanne Spector

CPSIA information can be obtained
at www.ICGtesting.com
Printed in the USA
JSHW062336161122
33328JS00003B/3